RELIGION IN AMERICAN
PUBLIC LAW

RELIGION IN AMERICAN PUBLIC
LAW

DAVID FELLMAN
Professor of Political Science
University of Wisconsin

Boston University Press

The Gaspar G. Bacon Lectures on the Constitution of
the United States

LIBRARY OF CONGRESS CATALOG CARD NO. 65-17006
PRINTED IN THE UNITED STATES OF AMERICA

FOR ROBERTA

THE BACON LECTURESHIP

The Gaspar G. Bacon Lectureship on the Constitution of the United States was established in 1927 by Mrs. Robert Bacon of New York in honor of her son, at that time Secretary of the Board of Trustees of Boston University. After several terms in the Massachusetts General Court (legislature) and two years as Lieutenant Governor, Gaspar G. Bacon retired from active politics and joined the Department of Government, College of Liberal Arts at Boston University in 1938. His teaching career was interrupted by four years of service in World War II. September 1947 found Professor Bacon back at Boston University, but only for a short period which ended suddenly with his death on Christmas Day.

David Fellman, Professor of Political Science at the University of Wisconsin, was invited to be the guest lecturer for the academic year of 1963-64. Professor Fellman's annual analysis of United States Supreme Court decisions which appears in the *American Political Science Review* is anxiously awaited by scholars in the field. He is the author of *The Defendant's Rights* (1958); *The Limits of Freedom* (1959); and *The Supreme Court and Education* (1960). He is also a contributor to various legal and political science journals. Born in Omaha, Nebraska, he did his undergraduate work at the University of Nebraska and received his doctorate from Yale. He is presently President of the American Association of University Professors, and is a former Vice-President of the American Political Science Association. He received the Governmental Affairs Award from the Social Science Research Council in 1959-60, served on the Governor's Commission on Constitutional Revision for Wisconsin in 1960, and is a member of the Governor's Commission on Human Rights.

THE BACON LECTURESHIP

CONTENTS

RELIGION IN AMERICAN PUBLIC LAW

I

It is well that people should gather together occasionally to discuss serious, controversial questions of public policy. Speaking at a recent seminar on the subject of religion and freedom, Father Thomas Gilby, a Dominican friar, observed that "civilization is formed by men locked together in argument. From this dialogue, the community becomes a political community."[1] It is in this spirit, and with this objective, that I shall undertake to discuss a number of issues on which there are grave and deeply-felt differences of opinion. The state and the church are two of man's oldest, most powerful, and most pervasive institutions. When they collide, as they often do, sparks are bound to fly. Both institutions command tremendous loyalties, and both have mustered over the years of history impassioned critics and opponents, as well as devoted friends and supporters.

Nevertheless, as we approach the subject of the place of the state and religion in American public law, we may take comfort in observing that with all of our differences there is a broad concensus in which most Americans have achieved a great deal of common ground.

In the last edition of Cooley's *Constitutional Limitations*,[2] probably the most influential treatise ever written in the field of American constitutional law,[3] the learned author states:

> A careful examination of the American constitutions will disclose the fact that nothing is more fully set forth or more plainly expressed than the determination of their authors to preserve and perpetuate religious liberty, and to guard against the slightest approach towards the establishment of an inequality in the civil and political rights of citizens, which shall have for its basis only their differences of religious belief. The American people came to the work of framing their fundamental laws, after centuries of religious oppression and persecution, sometimes by one party or sect and sometimes by another, had taught them the utter futility of all attempts to propagate religious opinions by the rewards, penalties, or terrors of human law. They could not fail to perceive, also, that a union of Church and State, like that which existed in England, if not wholly impracticable in America, was certainly opposed to the

---

[1] McDonald, Report on Religion and Freedom, on a seminar sponsored by the Fund for the Republic, 1958, p. 6.
[2] 2 Cooley, A Treatise on Constitutional Limitations 960 (8th ed. 1927).
[3] See Twiss, Lawyers and the Constitution ch. 2 (1942); Jacobs, Law Writers and the Constitution passim (1954).

spirit of our institutions, and that any domineering of one sect over another was repressing to the energies of the people, and must necessarily tend to discontent and disorder. Whatever, therefore, may have been their individual sentiments upon religious questions, or upon the propriety of the State assuming supervision and control of religious affairs under other circumstances, the general voice has been, that persons of every religious persuasion should be made equal before the law, and that questions of religious belief and religious worship should be questions between each individual man and his Maker.

I think that this statement from Cooley's treatise would meet with general approval. There can be no doubt that religious liberty, and the correlative doctrine of separation of church and state, are deeply rooted in the American constitutional experience. The first amendment to the United States Constitution declares that "Congress shall make no law respecting an establishment of religion, or prohibiting the free exercise thereof." The third clause of article VI provides that "no religious test shall ever be required as a qualification to any office or public trust under the United States." While the first amendment applies only to the national government,[4] the fourteenth amendment, which was ratified in 1868, stipulates that no state shall deprive anyone of his liberty without due process of law. In gradually expanding the "new liberty"[5] of the fourteenth amendment to include first amendment rights—beginning with the incorporation of the free speech guaranty in 1925[6]—the Court finally ruled squarely in 1940, in *Cantwell v. Connecticut*,[7] that the liberty of religion is one of the component elements of the liberty which the due process clause of the Constitution protects against state violation. In addition, both the concept of religious freedom and that of separation of church and state are spelled out in the state constitutions, generally in greater detail than in the federal document. That there is a powerful American commitment to both concepts can admit of no doubt.

Some writers have called freedom of speech "the first freedom,"[8] and in an important sense it may well be such, because freedom of speech must exist if men are to be able to defend any of their other freedoms.[9]

---

[4] Permoli v. New Orleans, 44 U.S. (3 How.) 589 (1845). Justice Catron said: "The constitution makes no provision for protecting the citizens of the respective States in their religious liberties; this is left to the state constitutions and laws; nor is there any inhibition imposed by the constitution of the United States in this respect on the States." Id. at 609.

[5] See Warren, The New "Liberty" under the Fourteenth Amendment, 39 Harv. L. Rev. 431 (1926).

[6] Gitlow v. New York, 268 U.S. 652 (1925).

[7] 310 U.S. 296 (1940).

[8] See Ernst, The First Freedom (1946).

[9] Justice Cardozo once said of freedom of thought and speech that "one may say that it is the matrix, the indispensable condition, of nearly every other form of freedom." Palko v. Connecticut, 302 U.S. 319, 327 (1937).

But if priority is based upon considerations of time alone, religious freedom may well be regarded as having come first, for it is in the area of religious belief and worship that man in the emergent modern world first staked out a claim to the free exercise of an important right which the state may not lawfully invade.

The case for religious freedom has been made so often, by so many, that the principal lines of argument are now pretty well taken for granted. Perhaps the most celebrated statement of reasons for the guaranty of religious liberty is still to be found in Virginia's *Act for Establishing Religious Freedom*, which Thomas Jefferson presented to the legislature of his state in 1779, and which was adopted seven years later.[10] In the preamble to the act, Jefferson noted that since God had created the mind free, "all attempts to influence it by temporal punishments or burdens, or by incapacitations, tend only to beget habits of hypocrisy and meanness." Thus coercion of belief is futile. In addition, he pointed out that legislators and rulers, civil as well as ecclesiastical, are themselves "but fallible and uninspired men," and thus in no position to set up their particular modes of thinking as being the only true and infallible opinions, and impose them upon others. Through all time, throughout the world, this has only resulted in the establishment and maintenance of false religions. In addition, Jefferson maintained that it was "sinful and tyrannical" to compel a man to contribute money for the propagation of opinions which he disbelieves. It would even be wrong to force a man to support a minister of his own religious persuasion, since that would deprive him of the liberty to support the particular pastor of whom he most approves. He added that compulsory support would have the unhappy result of removing from the pastor necessary incentives to win approval through "earnest and unremitting labors."[11] Our civil rights, he said, "have no dependence on our religious opinions," from which it follows that it is wholly wrong to deny anyone access to public office because of his religious opinions. Furthermore, "it tends also to corrupt the principles of that very religion it is meant

---

10 For the text see Cornerstones of Religious Freedom in America 74-75 (Blau ed. 1949).

11 In his Notes on Virginia (1781), Jefferson remarked that support of the Anglican Church in Virginia had "begotten . . . indolence in its clergy." Cornerstones of Religious Freedom in America, op. cit. supra note 10, at 76-77. It is of interest to note that the present Constitution of Rhode Island, which dates from 1843, in the clause which guarantees religious freedom states the case for religious freedom in classic Jeffersonian terms, as follows: "Whereas Almighty God hath created the mind free; and all attempts to influence it by temporal punishments or burdens, or by civil incapacitations, tend to beget habits of hypocrisy and meanness; and whereas a principal object of our venerable ancestors, in their migration to this country and their settlement of this state was, as they expressed it, to hold forth a lively experiment, that a flourishing civil state may stand and be best maintained with full liberty in religious concernments: We, therefore, declare . . . ." R.I. Const. art. I, § 3.

to encourage, by bribing, with a monopoly of worldly honors and emoluments, those who will externally profess and conform to it." It is "a dangerous fallacy, which at once destroys all religious liberty," to permit the civil magistrate to extend his authority into the field of opinion, because since he is the judge of what is right or wrong, the rule guiding judgment will be merely his own opinion. "It is time enough for the rightful purposes of civil government," Jefferson declared, "for its officers to interfere when principles break out into overt acts against peace and good order." And finally, he said, "truth is great and will prevail if left to herself, that she is the proper and sufficient antagonist to error, and has nothing to fear from the conflict, unless by human interposition disarmed of her natural weapons, free argument and debate, errors ceasing to be dangerous when it is permitted freely to contradict them."

In his *Notes of Virginia* Jefferson maintained that man has never submitted, and could not submit, his rights of conscience to the authority of his rulers, since we are answerable for them only to God. "The legitimate powers of government," he wrote, "extend to such acts only as are injurious to others. But it does me no injury to say there are twenty gods, or no God. It neither picks my pocket nor breaks my leg."[12] Coercion breeds hypocrisy and, indeed, strengthens man's commitment to error. "Reason and free inquiry are the only effectual agents against error." For, he asked, "What has been the effect of coercion? To make one half the world fools, and the other half hypocrites."[13]

The arguments for the separation of church and state are equally well-known through many years of repetition. In his *Memorial and Remonstrance on the Religious Rights of Man*, published in 1784 in the campaign against a bill for the support of teachers of the Christian religion through public taxation, James Madison made out a very persuasive case. Arguing that religion can be directed only by reason and conviction, and not by force or violence, and must therefore be left to the conviction and conscience of every man, he maintained that the notion that the civil magistrate is a competent judge of truth is "an arrogant pretension, falsified by the contradictory opinions of rulers in all ages, and throughout the world."[14] The notion that the civil magistrate may employ religion "as an engine of civil policy" Madison regarded as "an unhallowed perversion of the means of salvation." He declared that the Christian religion did not need the establishment proposed by the bill, because it is not dependent upon the powers of this world. It is well-known that religion has flourished without the support of man-made laws, and indeed, in the teeth of opposition from them. In fact, since

---

[12] Cornerstones of Religious Freedom in America, op. cit. supra note 10, at 78.
[13] Id. at 79.
[14] Id. at 83.

religion must have existed before human policy was formulated, it exists independently of such policy. Religious establishments have in the past hurt religion. "What have been its fruits?" he asked. And he replied: "More or less, in all places, pride and indolence in the clergy; ignorance and servility in the laity; in both, superstition, bigotry, and persecution."[15] On the other hand, Madison maintained that establishment was not necessary for the support of civil government, and that in this respect the influence of established religions has been bad. They have been used to erect spiritual tyrannies or they have served as the support for political tyranny. A just government does not require the support of religion, since it is "best supported by protecting every citizen in the enjoyment of his religion with the same equal hand that protects his person and property. . . ."[16]

Summarizing Madison's views, Justice Rutledge once wrote:

As the Remonstrance discloses throughout, Madison opposed every form and degree of official relation between religion and civil authority. For him religion was a wholly private matter beyond the scope of civil power either to restrain or to support. Denial or abridgment of religious freedom was a violation of rights both of conscience and of natural equality. State aid was no less obnoxious or destructive to freedom and to religion itself than other forms of state interference.... With Jefferson, Madison believed that to tolerate any fragment of establishment would be by so much to perpetuate restraint upon that freedom. Hence he sought to tear out the institution not partially but root and branch, and to bar its return forever.

In no phase was he more unrelenting absolute than in opposing state support or aid by taxation. Not even "three pence" contribution was thus to be exacted from any citizen for such a purpose. . . . Tithes had been the lifeblood of establishment before and after other compulsions disappeared. Madison and his coworkers made no exceptions or abridgments to the complete separation they created. Their objection was not to small tithes. It was to any tithes whatsoever.[17]

Madison's views on this subject have always been accorded special weight. With George Mason he was co-author of the clause on religion of Virginia's landmark Declaration of Rights of 1776. He was an enthusiastic supporter of Jefferson's Bill for Establishing Religious Freedom, and after Jefferson left for Europe in 1784 its principal sponsor. He led the fight against the Assessment Bill during the legislative struggle of 1784-1785 in Virginia. As a member of the First Congress he was the prime author of the Bill of Rights. In phrasing the first amendment, Mr. Irving Brant, Madison's leading biographer, has as-

[15] Id. at 84.
[16] Id. at 84-85.
[17] Everson v. Board of Educ., 330 U.S. 1, 39-41 (1947) (dissenting opinion).

serted that Madison's aim "was to strike down financial aid to religious institutions out of the public purse. . . . Not by the most microscopic concession would he deviate from absolute separation between 'the authority of human laws and the natural rights of man.' "[18] Indeed, as President, Madison took very extreme positions indeed. He vetoed a bill to incorporate the Protestant Episcopal Church in the District of Columbia. He also vetoed a bill for the relief of the Baptist Church in the Mississippi Territory by giving it a parcel of land. He even expressed opposition to having chaplains in Congress or in the armed forces, and he did not think that Presidents should issue religious proclamations. Clearly Madison took the concept of separation quite literally.

There has long been a conviction in our country that the separation of church and state has had a favorable influence upon the condition of religion. Long ago De Tocqueville observed that in America the churches have influence instead of power and that they were in a very healthy condition as compared with the situation in Europe, where the weakness of religion was due to its intimate connection with the state.[19] He said that he spoke to several priests about the astonishing strength of religion in the United States. "I found," he wrote, "that they differed upon matters of detail alone, and that they all attributed the peaceful dominion of religion in their country mainly to the separation of church and state. I do not hesitate to affirm that during my stay in America I did not meet a single individual, of the clergy or the laity, who was not of the same opinion on this point."[20]

An interesting illustration of the same point of view with respect to the place of the concept of separation of church and state in the United States was suggested by an episode at a sitting of the Ecumenical Council Vatican II in late October, 1963.[21] Acting collectively for the first time at the resumed Council meeting, the 236 Roman Catholic Bishops of the United States indicated that they objected to the use, in a document on the nature of the church ("De Ecclesia") of the adjective "infaustae"—which may be translated as "unfortunate" or "regrettable" —as a description of the concept of the separation of church and state. While they conceded that the association of the word with the concept might be based on a misunderstanding of a clause of the text under debate, they indicated that they wanted not the slightest doubt on the matter. They were apparently not satisfied with the explanation that the word "infaustae" applied only to "separation by oppression." One of their spokesmen, Bishop Victor Reed of Oklahoma City and Tulsa,

[18] Brant, James Madison the Nationalist 1780-1787, pp. 353-54 (1948).
[19] 1 De Tocqueville, Democracy in America 300-14 (Bradley ed. 1948).
[20] Id. at 308.
[21] My account here is based on a news story written by Milton Backer for the New York Times, October 24, 1963, p. 12.

declared that the American Bishops objected to the adjective because "the American [Roman Catholic] church is in favor of separation of church and state," and because the word in question might convey a contrary impression to the American public. Of course, this still leaves open the question as to the particular meaning which is ascribed to the concept of separation, but it is very significant that the American Bishops insisted upon objecting to a phrase which suggested general hostility to the whole idea.

Long after De Tocqueville wrote his great treatise on democracy in America, another distinguished visitor to our shores, Lord Bryce, made similar observations about what he described as an axiom accepted "by all Americans that the civil power ought to be not only neutral and impartial as between different forms of faith, but ought to leave these matters entirely on one side, regarding them no more than it regards the artistic or literary pursuits of the citizen."[22] And he went on to say: "There seem to be no two opinions on this subject in the United States. Even the Protestant Episcopal clergy, who are in many ways disposed to admire and feel with their brethren in England; even the Roman Catholic bishops, whose creed justifies the enforcement of the true faith by the secular arm, assure the European visitor that if State establishment were offered them they would decline it, preferring the freedom they enjoy to any advantages the State could confer. Every religious community can now organize itself in whatever way it pleases, lay down its own rules of faith and discipline, create and administer its own system of judicature, raise and apply its funds at its uncontrolled discretion. A church established by the State would not be able to do all these things, because it would also be controlled by the State, and it would be exposed to the envy and jealousy of other sects."

In short, the concept of the separation of church and state rests upon a conviction that separation is good for the church, which should not be dependent upon the state, and good for the state, which should not be involved in religious controversy. Then there is the purely prudential consideration that in a country with over 250 different religions or sects government cannot afford to take anything but a neutral position. The sheer multiplicity of sects requires government to be as neutral as it can possibly be, if only to keep the peace. A very good reason, though by no means the only one, for excluding religious teaching from the public schools is the desire to avoid sectarian conflict. Thus John Dewey once pointed out that the separation of state and church in the American tradition was not due to indifference or hostility to religion. "The cause," he wrote, "lay largely in the diversity and vitality of the various denominations, each fairly sure that, with a fair field and no favor, it

---

[22] 2 Bryce, The American Commonwealth 766 (Rev. ed. 1913).

could make its own way; and each animated by a jealous fear that, if any connection of State and Church were permitted, some rival denomination would get an unfair advantage."[23]

The concept of separation, however, rests upon other than dictates of prudence. Our political theory rejects the Hegelian notion that the state is the march of God upon the earth. We have developed a concept of the limited state, according to which many important activities and interests of a complex society are outside its scope. The state, with us, is neither omnicompetent nor omniscient. Furthermore, since the church is a spiritual body, and the state is a worldly institution, they have different purposes and different functions.[24] It was on some such assumption that such men as Roger Williams and Jonathan Edwards maintained that the state has no jurisdiction over religion. Deist and humanist groups in the eighteenth century, starting from different assumptions about the nature of religion, reached similar conclusions about the relations between state and church. James Madison thought that religion is outside the jurisdiction of government because matters of conscience are all voluntary in character. No one, in his view, can in the nature of things be compelled by the state to believe in or profess a religious faith. It has long been believed in this country that the inalienable rights of conscience "are of too high a rank and dignity," in the words of a representative Baptist at the time of the American Revolution, "to be submitted to the decrees of councils, or the imperfect laws of fallible legislators."[25] And he added: "Religion is a concern between God and the soul with which no human authority can intermeddle . . . ." Equally important has been the notion that when religion gets mixed up with the state "it may be constrained," as De Tocqueville pointed out, "to defend allies whom its interests, and not the principle of love, have given to it . . . . The church cannot share the temporal power of the state without being the object of a portion of that animosity which the latter excites."[26] He went on to observe that "when religion clings to the interests of the world, it becomes almost as fragile a thing as the powers of earth. It is the only one of them all which can hope for immortality; but if it be connected with their ephemeral power, it shares

---

[23] Intelligence in the Modern World 706 (Ratner ed. 1939).

[24] In his famous "address" to the Baptist Association of Danbury, Jefferson declared that "religion is a matter which lies solely between man and his God, that he owes account to none other for his faith or his worship, that the legislative powers of government reach actions only, and not opinions . . . ." 16 Jefferson's Works 281 (Monticello ed. 1903).

[25] Isaac Backus, in a petition against a Massachusetts precinct tax for the support of the Established Church, 1774, quoted in Pfeffer, Church, State, and Freedom 89 (1953).

[26] Pfeffer, op. cit. supra note 25, at 310.

their fortunes and may fall with those transient passions which alone supported them."[27]

II

The American commitment to the twin principles of freedom of religion and separation of church and state is very widely accepted; it is deeply rooted in our historical experience; and it is supported by powerfully cogent considerations. But to comprehend the actual dimensions of these principles in a workaday world, it is essential to go beyond these generalizations. In actual fact, neither concept under consideration is a simple one, and neither can be stated in absolute terms. Freedom of religion is one of civilized man's most cherished freedoms, but it is not and cannot be without limit. While man may be completely free to believe whatever he chooses to accept in matters of religious faith, he is not at liberty to act as he pleases merely by appending a religious label to his act. Similarly, while the separation of church and state is most desirable, for very weighty reasons, I shall argue that a complete and uncompromising separation is, in the nature of things, altogether unattainable. We are confronted with grave problems in this field of religion and the state, but I do not believe that we can find many viable solutions by standing on absolutist presuppositions. Only if we eschew extremism and fanaticism can we hope to make the necessary adjustments which lead to tolerable conclusions.

It is an axiom of American constitutional law that no right is absolute. Capital punishment and wartime military conscription testify to the fact that not even the right to life itself is absolute. The tens of thousands of people now residing in our jails are vivid proof of the fact that at many points liberty shades into license. Justice Field once stated this point very clearly in an impressive opinion dealing with the power of the state to control or regulate the uses of property.[28] He wrote:

> It is undoubtedly true that it is the right of every citizen of the United States to pursue any lawful trade or business . . . . But the possession and enjoyment of all rights are subject to such reasonable conditions as may be deemed by the governing authority of the country essential to the safety, health, peace, good order and morals of the community. Even liberty itself, the greatest of all rights, is not unrestricted license to act according to one's own will. It is only freedom from restraint under conditions essential to the equal enjoyment of the same right by others. It is then liberty regulated by law.

---

[27] Id. at 311.
[28] Crowley v. Christensen, 137 U.S. 86, 89-90 (1890). For an extended philosophical analysis of this point see Willoughby, The Ethical Basis of Political Authority (1930).

There are some people, including even a sitting Supreme Court Justice,[29] who believe or profess to believe in the conception of absolute rights or liberties. But the concept of absolute rights is untenable, for a number of reasons which I find highly persuasive. For one thing, if we conceded the possibility of absolute rights, then we could have only one at the same time, for if we had as many as two at the same time, and one conflicted with the other, then a choice would have to be made, and one absolute right would turn out to be less absolute than the other. Furthermore, in a legal system which includes a considerable number of rights, one must yield to another in any case where the principles themselves collide with each other. To cite a familiar example, where a newspaper gets into difficulties with a court for publishing something about a pending case which is regarded as improper by the law, the litigant's right to a fair trial may be preferred to the newsman's freedom of the press.[30] This does not mean that there is no such thing as the right to freedom of the press, or that it is unimportant. It merely means that in some situations it may seem best to have it yield to some other significant right. But the right to a fair trial is not couched in absolute terms either, for even such a basic or elemental aspect of the concept as the right of the accused to be present at every stage of his trial may yield to other considerations. Thus the Supreme Court once held that a criminal trial was not constitutionally deficient because the defendant was not allowed to go along with the judge, jury and counsel when they went out of the courtroom to view the actual scene of the crime.[31]

Finally, the interest of society in protecting the rights of the individual often conflict with other interests which society also cherishes and seeks to protect, and when this happens choices must be made. A classic example is the law of libel. Here society's concern for protecting reputation prevails over claims to free speech.[32] Similarly freedom of the press may be required to yield to the community's right to protect public morals from the debasement of hard-core obscenity.[33] Thus, Mr. Justice Roberts once wrote, "No one would have the hardihood to suggest that the principle of freedom of speech sanctions incitement to riot or

---

[29] See Black & Cahn, Justice Black and First Amendment "Absolutes": A Public Interview, 37 N.Y.U.L. Rev. 549 (1962); Black, The Bill of Rights, 35 N.Y.U.L. Rev. 865 (1960). See also Meiklejohn, Political Freedom (1960).

[30] See Craig v. Harney, 331 U.S. 367 (1947); Pennekamp v. Florida, 328 U.S. 331 (1946); Bridges v. California, 314 U.S. 252 (1941).

[31] Snyder v. Massachusetts, 291 U.S. 97 (1934). Justice Cardozo observed: "A fertile source of perversion in constitutional theory is the tyranny of labels." Id. at 114. And: "Due process of law requires that the proceedings shall be fair, but fairness is a relative, not an absolute concept. It is fairness with reference to particular conditions or particular results." Id. at 116.

[32] See Beauharnais v. Illinois, 343 U.S. 250 (1952).

[33] See Roth v. United States, 354 U.S. 476 (1957).

that religious liberty connotes the privilege to exhort others to physical attack upon those belonging to another sect. When clear and present danger of riot, disorder, interference with traffic upon the public streets, or other immediate threat to public safety, peace, or order, appears, the power of the State to prevent or punish is obvious."[34] Similarly, Justice Murphy, a very staunch defender of civil liberties, stated flatly:

> Allowing the broadest scope to the language and purpose of the Fourteenth Amendment, it is well understood that the right of free speech is not absolute at all times and under all circumstances. There are certain well-defined and narrowly limited classes of speech, the prevention and punishment of which has never been thought to raise any Constitutional problem. These include the lewd and obscene, the profane, the libelous, and the insulting or "fighting" words—those which by their very utterance inflict injury or tend to incite an immediate breach of the peace. It has been well observed that such utterances are no essential part of any exposition of ideas, and are of such slight social value as a step to truth that any benefit that may be derived from them is clearly outweighed by the social interest in order and morality.[35]

I think that in all branches of American constitutional law, the most difficult intellectual problem is to locate the point at which one legal right, or doctrine or interest must appropriately yield to another. Many different formulas are used in different situations. Thus the right of free speech gives way when speech poses a clear and present danger to what society regards as its vital security interests.[36] Our judges have long been struggling with the problem of drawing a line between reasonable searches and seizures, which are permissible, and unreasonable searches and seizures, which are forbidden by the Constitution.[37] The same problem exists in branches of American constitutional law which are not concerned with civil liberties. Thus, ever since its decision in the famous case of *Cooley v. Board of Wardens*,[38] the Supreme Court has been trying to draw the line between permissible and forbidden regulation by the states of interstate commerce in situations where Congress has been silent. The *Cooley* principle is that in the absence of federal action, states may regulate those aspects of interstate commerce where the desirability of local diversity outweighs the necessity for a uniform national policy. As Chief Justice Stone observed in a leading case, the problem is one of accommodating "the competing demands of

---

[34] Cantwell v. Connecticut, 310 U.S. 296, 308 (1940).
[35] Chaplinsky v. New Hampshire, 315 U.S. 568, 571-72 (1942).
[36] See Yates v. United States, 354 U.S. 298 (1957) ; Dennis v. United States, 341 U.S. 494 (1951).
[37] See the debates among the Justices in recent cases where they divided sharply, as in Frank v. Maryland, 359 U.S. 360 (1959) ; United States v. Rabinowitz, 339 U.S. 56 (1950) ; Harris v. United States, 331 U.S. 145 (1947).
[38] 53 U.S. (12 How.) 299 (1851).

the state and national interests involved."[39] I believe that the *Cooley* rule, which the Court arrived at only after a long period of fumbling with other possible formulations, is a sensible rule where the overriding purpose is to discover in concrete situations a reasonable point of equilibrium between localism and centralism, both of which we prize greatly.

These various tests are, to be sure, vague and imprecise. The Court is not an IBM machine which supplies the correct answers when the punch cards are fed into it. While efforts are being made by some political scientists to bring greater precision to judicial decision-making through methods of quantification,[40] and while it may well be that something useful will some day come out of these efforts, I see no present way of avoiding the exercise of rational judgment in making decisions in law suits between adversary parties asserting legal rights. I recently heard an American political scientist of great distinction argue that we could achieve greater precision and predictability in our public law if only we had a truly coherent national political philosophy. I regard this as a rather sophisticated way of seeking to discover what has been for so many for so long a time the holy grail of some legal philosophers, the legal slot machine. Perhaps we can indulge ourselves, once in a while, in the wistful search for precise and accurate formulas which will reduce our reliance upon the human mind's exercise of rational judgment. But I have never been able to conjure up the image of a truly coherent national political philosophy which would make decision-making automatic or even quasi-automatic. As Justice Cardozo once observed in one of his great lectures, political and social science has not yet "formulated a conception of liberty so precise and accurate that, applied as a touchstone by the courts, it will mechanically disclose the truth."[41] But he also thought it was desirable for judges and legal scholars to be informed about the history and philosophy of the problems they grapple with. "I do suggest and believe," he wrote, "that empirical solutions will be saner and sounder if in the background of the empiricism there is the study and the knowledge of what men have thought and written in the anxious search and groping for a co-ordinating principle."[42]

Justice Holmes once remarked that "constitutional law like other mortal contrivances has to take some chances . . . ."[43] I think that

---

[39] Parker v. Brown, 317 U.S. 341, 362 (1943).

[40] For a review of the literature in this area by its leading exponent, see Judicial Decision-Making (Schubert ed. 1963); Schubert, Behavioral Research in Public Law, 57 Am. Pol. Sci. Rev. 433 (1963). For a critique of this school of thought see Mendelson, The Neo-Behavioral Approach to the Judicial Process: A Critique, 57 Am. Pol. Sci. Rev. 593 (1963).

[41] Cardozo, The Paradoxes of Legal Science, 96-97 (1928).

[42] Id. at 97.

[43] Blinn v. Nelson, 222 U.S. 1, 7 (1911).

this is an important truth. Public law is not an exact or even very precise science. Perhaps it should be such; it may well be that we would be better off if it were. One may even speculate that our present-day quantifiers will some day succeed in reducing judicial decision-making to wholly mathematical formulas. But this has not happened yet, and I see no present alternative to the exercise by judges, lawyers and scholars of rational judgment in resolving justiciable disputes in adversary proceedings. Even in the field of human rights, where the law expresses its greatest concern for the integrity of the individual, and his freedom from physical and intellectual restraints, we cannot and we should not and we will not be permitted to ignore the pull of countervailing social considerations. As Justice Cardozo once observed, in his own pithy way, "justice, though due to the accused, is due to the accuser also. The concept of fairness must not be strained till it is narrowed to a filament. We are to keep the balance true."[44]

I know that this conception of constitutional law stirs some people to anger, and many more to a fretful state of impatience. The desire for greater precision in the formulation of principles and a larger measure of predictability in applying principles to concrete factual situations, is wholly understandable. On purely theoretical grounds I cannot say that I feel opposed to such thinking. In fact, it is precisely the task of legal scholars to sharpen up our intellectual tools and promote predictability in the law through careful and clarifying analysis of legal doctrines. Their scholarship should cover a wide range of inquiry, including historical antecedents, the flow of precedents, the requirements of logical analysis, and the objective facts of the workaday world. But, at least with our present tools of thought, it is a snare and a delusion to think we can formulate rules with such precision that we can rule out the exercise of rational judgment on the part of our judges. This means that we must recognize that judges will not and cannot be expected to make decisions without taking thought and without weighing one consideration against another. I refuse to be terrified about the possibility of our developing a legal system where a machine punches out the "right" solution to a legal problem mechanically, or where a mathematical formula supplies an answer which is "correct" as far as three decimal points. I do not believe Orwell's 1984 nightmare is going to come about in the field of American constitutional law, at least not in the predictable future. Beyond that point in time my crystal ball gets so clouded as to become quite unreliable.

III

Freedom of religion is absolute, I should suppose, only in the sense that one is free to believe anything at all. The flourishing of what strikes

---

[44] Snyder v. Massachusetts, 291 U.S. 97, 122 (1934).

14

most people as rather strange brands of religion, in the world of the small cults,[45] would seem to attest to this fact. Over a century ago, De Tocqueville noticed how many "strange sects" we had in this country, many of them devoted to various brands of fanatical spiritualism, and he observed that apparently "religious insanity is very common in the United States."[46] But religion involves more than various systems of belief; it invariably involves action as well, ranging from mere ceremonial to the practice of medicine, and wherever the practice of religion goes beyond mere belief, and deleterious social consequences are encountered, then our constitutional law permits the state to step in. Justice Roberts pointed out in *Cantwell v. Connecticut*[47] that the first amendment guaranty "embraces two concepts,—freedom to believe and freedom to act. The first is absolute but, in the nature of things, the second cannot be. Conduct remains subject to regulation for the protection of society." Thomas Jefferson, who was more strongly committed to religious liberty than to any other liberty,[48] took this same position. He once wrote to Madison that "the declaration that religious faith shall be unpunished does not give impunity to criminal acts dictated by religious error."[49]

As a matter of fact, no fewer than twenty-four of our state constitutions, in the very clauses which spell out the guaranty of religious freedom, go on to make the point that it is by no means without limit. Thus, ever since 1777,[50] the constitution of New York has guaranteed "the free exercise and enjoyment of religious profession and worship," but with the stated proviso that "the liberty of conscience hereby secured shall not be so construed as to excuse acts of licentiousness, or justify practices inconsistent with the peace or safety of this state."[51] This is a stock phrase which is incorporated in substantially this language in fifteen other state constitutions.[52] The Idaho constitution treats this subject more fully, for its Declaration of Rights not only declares that the liberty of conscience shall not be construed to excuse acts of licentiousness, but also that this guaranty cannot be used to justify "polyga-

---

[45] See Braden, These Also Believe (1949); Clark, The Small Sects in America (Rev. ed. 1949); Dohrman, California Cult (1958); 3 Stokes, Church and State in the United States 548-50 (1950).
[46] 2 De Tocqueville, op. cit. supra note 19, at 134.
[47] 310 U.S. 296, 303-04 (1940).
[48] See Levy, Jefferson and Civil Liberties (1963).
[49] 13 The Papers of Thomas Jefferson 442-43 (Boyd ed. 1950).
[50] N.Y. Const. of 1777, art. XXXVIII.
[51] N.Y. Const. art. I, § 3. The present wording of this section has been unchanged since 1894.
[52] See: Ariz. Const. art. II, § 12; Calif. Const. art. I, § 4; Colo. Const. art. II, § 4; Conn. Const. art. I, § 3; Fla. Const., Declaration of Rights, § 5; Ga. Const. art. I, § 1, para. 13; Ill. Const. art. II, § 3; Minn. Const. art. I, § 16; Miss. Const. art. III, § 18; Mo. Const. art. I, § 5; Nev. Const. art. I, § 1; N.D. Const. art. I, § 4; S.D. Const. art. VI, § 3; Wash. Const. art. I, § 11; Wyo. Const. art. I, § 18.

mous or other pernicious practices, inconsistent with morality or the peace or safety of the state," or to permit "any person, organization, or association to directly or indirectly aid or abet, counsel or advise any person to commit the crime of bigamy or polygamy, or any other crime."[53] The constitution of Maine says that every person has freedom of religion "provided he does not disturb the public peace, nor obstruct others in their religious worship," and demeans himself "peaceably."[54] The Maryland constitution assures each man religious freedom "unless, under color of religion, he shall disturb the good order, peace or safety of the State, or shall infringe the laws of morality, or injure others in their natural, civil or religious rights."[55]

Building Controls. It is, I think, altogether inevitable that the policies of the state should impinge upon the churches. The state is ubiquitous and all persons residing within it are subject, in some measure, to its control. It has tremendous responsibilities, ranging from the maintenance of law and order to the preservation of its independence through the conduct of foreign affairs and the maintenance of armed forces. It is concerned with the protection of morality and with public health and safety. It follows that there can be no such thing as a completely free church even in a free state, for the church is, of necessity, subject to the state in a variety of ways. To cite one specific example, a church must obey building codes and fire laws. The state seeks to protect people from unsafe buildings by prescribing minimum standards of safety. If a religious group erects a church edifice, it is equally obliged to put up a building whose walls will not collapse with the first strong wind. The fact that a building bears a religious label does not put it beyond the legitimate concern of government. Thus, when a church erects a building, the municipality may require it to take into consideration the necessity for off-street parking, for next to the problem of atomic war, parking is our most serious national concern today, and the state has a right to require the churches to take this into consideration when drawing up their building plans.[56]

---

[53] Idaho Const. art. I, § 4. A similar provision is in Mont. Const. art. III, § 4. The freedom of religion clause of the Oklahoma constitution expressly rules out plural marriages, art. I, § 2, as does the constitution of Utah art. III, § 1.

[54] Me. Const. art. I, § 3. For similar provisions see Mass. Const. Part I, art. II; N.H. Const. Part I, art. 5.

[55] Md. Const., Declaration of Rights, art. 36.

[56] See Allendale Congregation of Jehovah's Witnesses v. Grosman, 30 N.J. 273, 152 A.2d 569 (1959) ; Appeal of Trustees of Congregation of Jehovah's Witnesses, Bethel Unit, 183 Pa. Super. 219, 130 A.2d 240 (Super. Ct. 1957), appeal dismissed for want of a substantial federal question, 355 U.S. 40 (1957) ; State ex rel. Synod of Ohio of United Lutheran Church v. Joseph, 139 Ohio St. 229, 39 N.E.2d 515 (1942). The requirement of off-street parking must take into account the small size of the congregation, the condition of traffic during the hours of religious service, and the availability of space for parking on the streets. Board of Zoning Appeals v. Decatur, Ind. Co. of Jehovah's Witnesses, 233 Ind. 83, 117 N.E.2d 115 (1954).

16

In our increasingly crowded, urbanized society, government imposes many restrictions upon the uses of property, and many of them are as binding upon church property as upon any other, and for the same reasons. Thus it is established that a church is obliged to observe the set-back requirements of a municipal zoning ordinance, since these requirements are neither arbitrary nor capricious, and the churches, like other property owners, are reasonably able to comply.[57] The highest court of Michigan ruled in 1947 that a church installation consisting of tents, trailers and shacks could be abated as a nuisance.[58] The applicable ordinance permitted churches to be erected in zoned residential districts, but provided that all buildings must have windows, inside toilets, running water, sewage facilities, proper foundations, and similar amenities, and these regulations, the court asserted, serve proper police power purposes. The court also took into consideration that the religious group in question made so much noise in the early hours to 4 A.M. as to disturb others in the neighborhood. In fact, the court went so far as to assert that "the conclusion does not follow that every place in which religious services are conducted is a church."[59] In a general way, it is well established in the decisions of state appellate courts, that churches must obey laws relating to side yards,[60] sanitation and health, and fire hazards.[61] Some courts have gone so far as to enforce restrictive covenants which excluded churches from certain districts.[62]

A few courts have gone even further to take the position that a city may constitutionally zone against churches in residential areas, generally on the theory that a residential neighborhood may be allowed to preserve its character and property values by avoiding the increased traffic and noise which churches bring into the neighborhood.[63] This position,

[57] Board of Zoning Appeals v. Decatur, Ind. Co. of Jehovah's Witnesses, supra note 56.

[58] Portage Township v. Full Salvation Union, 318 Mich. 693, 29 N.W.2d 297 (1947), appeal dismissed, 333 U.S. 851 (1948).

[59] Id. at 700, 29 N.W.2d at 300.

[60] Kurman v. Philadelphia Zoning Bd. of Adjustment, 351 Pa. 247, 40 A.2d 381 (1945).

[61] Community Synagogue v. Bates, 1 N.Y.2d 445, 456, 136 N.E.2d 488, 495 (1956) (dictum); City of Sherman v. Simms, 143 Tex. 115, 183 S.W.2d 415 (1944).

[62] Bucklew v. Trustees Bayshore Baptist Church, 60 So. 2d 182 (Fla. 1952); Housing Authority v. Church of God, 401 Ill. 100, 81 N.E.2d 500 (1948); Christ's Methodist Church v. Macklanburg, 198 Okla. 297, 177 P.2d 1008 (1947).

[63] City of Chico v. First Ave. Baptist Church, 108 Cal. App. 2d 297, 238 P.2d 587 (3d Dist. 1951); Corporation of Presiding Bishop of Church of Jesus Christ of Latter-Day Saints v. City of Porterville, 90 Cal. App. 2d 656, 203 P.2d 823 (4th Dist. 1949), appeal dismissed for lack of a substantial federal question, 338 U.S. 805 (1949); West Hartford Methodist Church v. Zoning Bd. of Appeals, 143 Conn. 263, 121 A.2d 640 (1956); Miami Beach United Lutheran Church v. City of Miami Beach, 82 So. 2d 880 (Fla. 1955); Galfas v. Ailor, 81 Ga. App. 13, 57 S.E.2d 834 (1950); Jehovah's Witnesses v. Mullen, 214 Ore. 281, 330 P.2d 5 (1958).

however, is distinctly a minority position, for most state courts which have ruled on the question have refused to permit the exclusion of churches from residential areas, generally on the ground that such exclusion has no substantial relation to police power objectives.[64] The United States Supreme Court has never ruled on this question, but many state supreme courts have, and they have held repeatedly that a zoning ordinance or administrative decision under such an ordinance which excludes churches from residential areas is unconstitutional because it is arbitrary and unreasonable, since there is no substantial relation to public health, safety, morals or general welfare.[65] The same rule has been applied to the attempted exclusion of parochial schools from residential neighborhoods.[66] It is noted that churches are usually and customarily located in residential districts,[67] and that to relegate churches to business or manufacturing districts "could conceivably result in imposing a burden upon the free right to worship and, in some instances, in prohibiting altogether the exercise of that right."[68] Mere inconvenience to neighbors is not a convincing objection, because "the maintenance of churches is such a valuable right. . . ."[69] Since the church in this country is the teacher and guardian of morals, appellate judges have pointed out, one can hardly justify the exclusion of churches from residential neighborhoods for the purpose of protecting public morals.[70] In a recent case, the Court of Appeals of New York, taking into account "the high purposes, and the moral value," of

[64] See Yokley, Zoning Law and Practice § 222, at 110-12 (2d ed. 1953); Brindel, Zoning Out Religious Institutions, 32 Notre Dame Law. 627 (1957); Note, 70 Harv. L. Rev. 1428 (1957); Note, 27 St. John's L. Rev. 93 (1952).

[65] Ellsworth v. Gercke, 62 Ariz. 198, 156 P.2d 242 (1945); Board of Zoning Appeals v. Decatur, Ind. Co. of Jehovah's Witnesses, 233 Ind. 83, 117 N.E.2d 115 (1954); State ex rel. Westminster Church v. Building Inspector, 108 Neb. 859, 189 N.W. 617 (1922); Young Israel Organization v. Dworkin, 105 Ohio App. 89, 133 N.E.2d 174 (1956); State ex rel. Wenatchee Congregation of Jehovah's Witnesses v. City of Wenatchee, 50 Wash. 2d 378, 312 P.2d 195 (1957); State ex rel. Howell v. Meador, 109 W. Va. 368, 154 S.E. 876 (1930).

[66] In re O'Hara's Appeal, 389 Pa. 35, 131 A.2d 587 (1957); Roman Catholic Archbishop v. Baker, 140 Ore. 600, 15 P.2d 391, 395 (1932); "by all civilized peoples, an educational institution, whose curriculum complies with the state law, is considered an aid to the general welfare." Contra, State ex rel. Wisconsin Lutheran High School Conference v. Sinar, 267 Wis. 91, 65 N.W.2d 43 (1954).

[67] Congregation Temple Israel v. City of Creve Coeur, 320 S.W.2d 451 (Mo. Sup. Ct. 1959).

[68] City of Sherman v. Simms, 143 Tex. 115, 120, 183 S.W.2d 415, 417 (1944).

[69] Congregation Comm. v. City Council, 287 S.W.2d 700, 705 (Tex. Civ. App. 1956).

[70] State ex rel. Tampa Co. of Jehovah's Witnesses v. City of Tampa, 48 So. 2d 78 (Fla. 1950); Mooney v. Village of Orchard Lake, 333 Mich. 389, 53 N.W.2d 308 (1952); State ex rel. Anshe Chesed Congregation v. Bruggemeier, 97 Ohio App. 67, 115 N.E.2d 65 (1953). The court said in Congregation Comm. v. City Council, supra note 69, at 705: "The church in our American community has traditionally occupied the role of both teacher and guardian of morals. Restrictions against churches could therefore scarcely be predicated upon a purpose to protect public morals."

18

churches, rejected as being inadequate reasons for excluding them from residential neighborhoods: mere pecuniary loss to a few near-by property owners, loss of tax revenue to the community, and allegations about noise and added traffic hazards.[71] It has been noted that to accomplish its purposes a church should be integrated into the home life of the community it serves.[72] As for funerals, the Nevada Supreme Court once brushed aside this objection with the observation that "it is a matter of common knowledge that funeral services are frequently conducted in the finest as well as the less pretentious private homes. . . . Death is a part of our existence, and is as natural as life."[73]

Public Health and Morals. One of government's oldest functions, and most widely recognized as legitimate, is the regulation of conduct for the purpose of protecting public health and morals. In this area of vital public interest there are to be found many illustrations of the proposition that freedom of religion is not absolute, and that at some point, even though the act arises from religious principle or is regarded as a religious right or duty, its religious character does not automatically put it beyond control by the state. All would agree, I should suppose, that the classic case in point is *Reynolds v. United States,*[74] decided in 1878, in which the Supreme Court upheld the constitutionality of a federal statute which outlawed polygamy in the territories. This case involved George Reynolds, Brigham Young's private secretary, and unquestionably the practice of polygamy was regarded by the Mormons of that day as required and sanctioned by their religion. In a case decided in 1890,[75] in which the Court upheld a territorial statute forbid-

---

[71] Diocese of Rochester v. Planning Bd., 1 N.Y.2d 508, 136 N.E.2d 827, 154 N.Y.S.2d 849 (1956).

[72] State ex rel. Synod of Ohio of United Lutheran Church v. Joseph, 139 Ohio St. 229, 39 N.E.2d 515 (1942).

[73] Bishop of Reno v. Hill, 59 Nev. 231, 245, 90 P.2d 217, 222 (1939).

[74] 98 U.S. 145 (1878). See also Cannon v. United States, 116 U.S. 55 (1885), where the court upheld another conviction in a case involving a Mormon who continued to live with and support two women, but claimed he had intimate relations only with one. The court ruled that the word "cohabit" did not necessarily include the idea of sexual relations. Cf. Snow v. United States, 118 U.S. 346 (1886). In State v. Musser, 110 Utah 534, 175 P.2d 724 (1946), the court upheld a criminal conspiracy among practitioners of polygamy, but the Supreme Court reversed and remanded on the ground that the statute upon which the prosecution depended was unconstitutionally vague, Musser v. Utah, 333 U.S. 95 (1948). On the remand, the state court also held the statute invalid for vagueness, State v. Musser, 118 Utah 537, 233 P.2d 193 (1950). A later Utah statute forbidding polygamy was upheld by the Utah Supreme Court in State v. Barlow, 107 Utah 292, 153 P.2d 647 (1944), appeal dismissed for want of a substantial federal question, 324 U.S. 829 (1944); cf. State v. Jessup, 98 Utah 482, 100 P.2d 969 (1940). See West, Kingdom of the Saints (1957); Andersen, Polygamy in Utah, 5 Utah L. Rev. 381 (1957).

[75] Davis v. Beason, 133 U.S. 333 (1890). An act of Congress forbidding polygamists to vote in the Territory of Utah was upheld in Murphy v. Ramsey, 114 U.S. 15 (1885). An Idaho statute denying the right to vote to polygamists was upheld in Wooley v. Watkins, 2 Idaho 555, 22 Pac. 102 (1889).

ding polygamists to vote, Justice Field said that to call the advocacy of polygamy "a tenet of religion is to offend the common sense of mankind."[76] I should think that it is even more offensive to the common sense of mankind to deny that the Mormons' advocacy of polygamy was a tenet of their religion. Perhaps Justice Field meant that Mormonism was not even a religion, but that is even more offensive to common sense. I suspect that Justice Field came closer to the nub of the matter when he went on to say that "crime is not the less odious because sanctioned by what any particular sect may designate as religion."[77] This means that a crime is a crime even if it bears a religious tag.

This is precisely what the Court held in the *Reynolds* case. Chief Justice Waite declared, on the basis of historical evidence, that the first amendment deprived Congress of all legislative power "over mere opinion, but was left free to reach actions which were in violation of social duties or subversive of good order."[78] He pointed out that polygamy has always been odious to western nations, that it was always illegal under the common law, and that it has always been a crime in every state. Furthermore, whatever else marriage may be, it is a social institution and a civil contract which is regulated by law. Thus the Chief Justice concluded that "laws are made for the government of actions, and while they cannot interfere with mere religious belief and opinions, they may with practices. Suppose one believed that human sacrifices were a necessary part of religious worship, would it be seriously contended that the civil government under which he lived could not interfere to prevent a sacrifice? Or if a wife religiously believed it was her duty to burn herself upon the funeral pile of her dead husband, would it be beyond the power of the civil government to prevent her carrying her belief into practice?"[79] Similarly, Justice Field declared in the 1890 case that "it was never intended or supposed that the [first] amendment could be invoked as a protection against legislation for the punishment of acts inimical to the peace, good order and morals of society. . . . However free the exercise of religion may be, it must be subordinate to the criminal laws of the country. . . ."[80] In another 1890 case,[81] another very eminent jurist, Justice Bradley, in an opinion sustaining an act of Congress which repealed Utah legislation incorporating the Mormon Church, pointed out that the charter of a church is not irrevocable merely because it is a religious and charitable institution. The decisive fact was that this church taught polygamy. "The existence of

---

76 Davis v. Beason, supra note 75, at 342.
77 Id. at 345.
78 Reynolds v. United States, 98 U.S. 145, 164 (1878).
79 Id. at 166.
80 Davis v. Beason, 133 U.S. 333, 342-43 (1890).
81 Mormon Church v. United States, 136 U.S. 1 (1890).

such a propaganda," Justice Bradley wrote, "is a blot on our civilization. The organization of a community for the spread and practice of polygamy is, in a measure, a return to barbarism. It is contrary to the spirit of Christianity and of all the civilization which Christianity has produced in the Western world."[82] He rejected the argument that the Mormons' practice of polygamy could be defended under the constitutional guaranty of religious freedom as "altogether a sophistical plea."[83] And Justice Bradley added: "The State has a perfect right to prohibit polygamy, and all other open offenses against the enlightened sentiment of mankind, notwithstanding the pretense of religious conviction by which they may be advocated and practiced."[84]

One of the last Supreme Court cases involving polygamy came up for decision in 1946.[85] It involved several members of a so-called Fundamentalist Mormon sect which, unlike the official Mormon Church,[86] not only believes in polygamy but actually practices it. Since plural wives had been transported across state lines, the federal government prosecuted for violation of the Mann Act, which makes it an offense to transport in interstate commerce "any woman or girl for the purpose of prostitution or debauchery, or for any other immoral purpose . . . ."[87] The question was whether the acts complained of in this case fell within the meaning of the phrase, "for any other immoral purpose." The Court sustained the convictions in this case, relying upon a well-known 1917 precedent which had established the proposition that the Mann Act was not restricted to commercialized sex.[88] Polygamy, said Justice Douglas, has long been outlawed in our society as "a notorious example of promiscuity." Above all, the Court brushed aside the argument that since the defendants had been motivated by a religious belief, the requisite criminal intent was lacking. "That defense," said Justice Douglas, "claims too much. If upheld, it would place beyond the law any act done under claim of religious sanction. But it has long been held that the fact that polygamy is supported by a religious creed affords no

---

[82] Id. at 49. Three justices dissented, not on the ground that Congress may not forbid polygamy in the territories, but because they had qualms about the confiscation of property.
[83] Id. at 49.
[84] Id. at 50. In Long v. State, 192 Ind. 524, 137 N.E. 49 (1922), religious belief was ruled out as a defense to a charge of bigamy.
[85] Cleveland v. United States, 329 U.S. 14 (1946). Conviction of a polygamist of violating the Federal Kidnapping Act, 18 U.S.C. § 1201 (1958), was set aside in Chatwin v. United States, 326 U.S. 455 (1946), on the ground that the facts would not support a finding of kidnapping. Justice Murphy pointed out, however, that "bona fide religious beliefs cannot absolve one from liability under the . . . Act . . . ." 326 U.S. at 460.
[86] The Mormon Church has forbidden polygamy since 1890. Toncray v. Budge, 14 Idaho 621, 95 Pac. 26 (1908).
[87] 18 U.S.C. § 2421 (1958).
[88] Caminetti v. United States, 242 U.S. 470 (1917).

defense in a prosecution for bigamy. . . . Whether an act is immoral within the meaning of the statute is not determined by the accused's concepts of morality. Congress has provided the standard."[89]

Public health and safety considerations often prevail over claims of religious belief and religious freedom. For example, compulsory vaccination of public school children has been held valid repeatedly by various appellate courts over religious objections.[90] The United States Supreme Court sustained compulsory vaccination for smallpox for the whole community, over religious and other objections, in a landmark case decided in 1905.[91] Similarly, a state university regulation requiring every student to take a chest X-ray examination has been upheld, even though the practice runs contrary to the student's religious convictions.[92] State courts have always registered approval of the fluoridation of public water where religious objections have been raised.[93] In fact, state supreme courts have gone even further to uphold state regulation or even prohibition of actual religious practices or ceremonials where public safety is clearly involved. This has occurred in connection with certain holiness cults which handle snakes in their religious worship.[94] State appellate courts have affirmed the validity of statutes which either regulate the manner in which the snakes shall be handled,[95] or prohibit their

[89] Cleveland v. United States, 329 U.S. 14, 20 (1946). Justices Black and Jackson dissented for the reason that they did not want to extend the dubious rule of the Caminetti case. Justice Murphy, in a separate dissenting opinion, argued that polygamy was not in the same class with prostitution and debauchery, and while he did not wish to defend it, he insisted that it was one of the basic forms of marriage, which, like other forms of marriage, was fundamentally a cultural institution rooted deeply in religious beliefs and social mores. He maintained that the Mann Act was aimed only at commercialized vice, and favored overruling the Caminetti decision, which he thought could not be justified on grounds of age alone.

[90] Zucht v. King, 260 U.S. 174 (1922) ; Anderson v. State, 84 Ga. App. 259, 65 S.E.2d 848 (1951) ; Vonnegut v. Baun, 206 Ind. 172, 188 N.E. 677 (1934) ; Mosier v. Barren County Bd. of Health, 308 Ky. 829, 215 S.W.2d 967 (1948) ; State v. Drew, 89 N.H. 54, 192 Atl. 629 (1937) ; Board of Educ. v. Maas, 56 N.J. Super. 245, 152 A.2d 393 (1959) ; Sadlock v. Board of Educ., 137 N.J.L. 85, 58 A.2d 218 (1948) ; State ex rel. Dunham v. Board of Educ., 154 Ohio St. 469, 96 N.E.2d 413 (1951), cert. denied, 341 U.S. 915 (1951) ; New Branfels v. Waldschmidt, 109 Tex. 302, 207 S.W. 303 (1918) ; see Comment, 26 U. Chi. L. Rev. 471 (1959).
[91] Jacobson v. Massachusetts, 197 U.S. 11 (1905).
[92] State ex rel. Holcomb v. Armstrong, 39 Wash. 2d 860, 239 P.2d 545 (1952). See Streich v. Board of Educ., 34 S.D. 169, 147 N.W. 779 (1914), which upheld, over religious objections, a requirement of a physical examination as a prerequisite to entering public school.
[93] De Aryan v. Butler, 119 Cal. App. 674, 260 P.2d 98 (4th Dist. 1953) ; Chapman v. Shreveport, 225 La. 859, 74 So. 2d 142 (1954) ; Kraus v. City of Cleveland, 116 N.E.2d 779 (Com. Pl. Ohio 1953), aff'd, 163 Ohio St. 559, 127 N.E.2d 609 (1955), appeal dismissed for want of a substantial federal question, 351 U.S. 935 (1956), noted in 3 St. Louis U.L.J. 284 (1955) ; Dowell v. City of Tulsa, 273 P.2d 859 (Okla. Sup. Ct. 1954), cert. denied, 348 U.S. 912 (1955) ; Baer v. City of Bend, 206 Ore. 221, 292 P.2d 134 (1956) ; see McNeil, The Fight for Fluoridation (1957) ; Nichols, Freedom of Religion and the Water Supply, 32 So. Cal. L. Rev. 158 (1959).
[94] See Womeldorf, Rattlesnake Religion, 64 The Christian Century 1517-18 (1947) ; Lake, Freedom to Worship Curiously, 1 U. Fla. L. Rev. 203 (1948).
[95] State v. Massey, 229 N.C. 734, 51 S.E.2d 179 (1949), appeal dismissed for

use altogether in connection with any religious service.[96] The Supreme Court of North Carolina said that the issue was simply whether the public safety or the defendants' religious practice comes first, and it declared without arguing the point that "the authorities are at one in holding that the safety of the public comes first."[97]

It is equally well established that the state may constitutionally regulate fortune telling, or the practice of communicating with departed spirits, even if it purports to be part of some religion. The Oklahoma Criminal Court of Appeals, in 1922, upheld the conviction of a "medium" who was a member of the National Spiritualist Association, and who claimed immunity on religious grounds from the operation of a statute which made fortune-telling illegal.[98] The Court could not make up its mind whether the defendant's system of belief was a religion or a mere piece of metaphysical speculation. But even if it is regarded as a religion, the Court noted that "religious liberty does not include the right to introduce and carry out every scheme or purpose which persons see fit to claim as a part of their religious system. No one can stretch his liberty so as to interfere with that of his neighbor, or violate police regulations or the penal laws of the land, enacted for the good order and general welfare of all the people."[99] In this instance the defendant told a young woman that she was speaking for Minnehaha, Longfellow's legendary Indian girl, and said that her patron would marry a rich man, and that sort of thing. This sounded very secular to the Court, and also as a "species of hypocrisy and legerdemain." "An innocent practice or entertainment," said the Court, "whether of a religious nature or not, may be regulated or suppressed where the tendencies and temptations to pervert it into evil channels is manifest, and where the evil is likely to overbalance the good. Fantastic philosophers and religious zealots, like other people, must conform to wholesome police regulations."[100] A waggish judge wrote a separate opinion in this case to indicate that he concurred "because the medium in question had never filed her schedule of rates with the state corporation commission."[101]

The Washington court has sustained the conviction of a medium who claimed to be a regularly ordained minister of the "National Astrological Society," for violating a statute which declared that anyone who

---

want of a substantial federal question, 336 U.S. 942 (1949) ; Harden v. State, 188 Tenn. 17, 216 S.W.2d 708 (1949).
[96] Lawson v. Commonwealth, 291 Ky. 437, 164 S.W.2d 972 (1942) ; Kirk v. Commonwealth, 186 Va. 839, 44 S.E.2d 409 (1947).
[97] State v. Massey, 229 N.C. 734, 51 S.E.2d 179 (1949).
[98] McMasters v. State, 21 Okla. Crim. 318, 207 Pac. 566 (1922).
[99] Id. at 323, 207 Pac. at 568.
[100] Id. at 325, 207 Pac. at 569.
[101] Id. at 328, 207 Pac. at 570.

asks for or receives compensation for practicing fortune-telling is a vagrant.[102] On the other hand, a New Jersey court once set aside the conviction of a medium who was attached to the First Spiritualist Church of Camden, under a statute which declared that the practitioner of fortune-telling is a disorderly person.[103] The court ruled that participation in a religious service was protected by the state constitutional guaranty of religious liberty where personal rights are not infringed, and laws relating to morality and property are not violated.

Whether the religious faith healer can be convicted of practicing medicine without a license presents a more complicated issue than fortune-telling. Clearly very many people believe that faith and prayer may heal. On the other hand, it is well established that the state may limit the practice of medicine, through licensing, to persons who have demonstrated their professional competence. In fact, all states do just this. Many state medical practice licensing laws seek to respect bona fide claims to religious liberty by providing that they do not apply to faith healing. Thus the New York statute specifies that it does not apply to or affect "the practice of religious tenets of any church."[104] Construing the statute, the New York Court of Appeals ruled, in 1916, that a Christian Science practitioner, operating within the rules of that church, could not be convicted of practicing medicine without a license.[105] The court stressed that the accused did not undertake to diagnose disease, or inquire into symptoms, or lay on the hands, or massage or otherwise manipulate the body. The court ruled that the legislature intended to exempt the Christian Science and other churches who believe that prayer to God cures. Nevertheless, the court warned that "the religious tenets of a church must be practiced in good faith to come within the exception. When such practice is fraud or pretense it is not excepted from the general prohibition. When wrong is practiced in the name of religion it is not protected by Constitution or statute."[106] The court also said that the question of whether the defendant was practicing the tenets of a recognized church within the meaning of the statutory exception was for the jury to decide.

The following year the New York Court of Appeals upheld the conviction of a spiritualist for illegal practice of medicine who claimed he was practicing the tenets of his church, but who for pay prescribed liniments and drugs for internal use.[107] Judge Cardozo pointed out in the opinion of the court that under the statute,

---

[102] State v. Neitzel, 69 Wash. 567, 125 Pac. 939 (1912).
[103] State v. DeLaney, 1 N.J. Misc. 619, 122 Atl. 890 (1923).
[104] N.Y. Educ. Law, § 6512(1)(h).
[105] People v. Cole, 219 N.Y. 98, 113 N.E. 790 (1916).
[106] Id. at 111, 113 N.E. at 794.
[107] People v. Vogelgesang, 221 N.Y. 290, 116 N.E. 977 (1917).

the profession and practice of the religion must be itself the cure. The sufferer's mind must be brought into submission to the infinite mind, and in this must be the healing. The operation of the power of spirit must be, not indirect and remote, but direct and immediate. If that were not so, a body of men who claimed divine inspiration might prescribe drugs and perform surgical operations under cover of the law. While the healer inculcates the faith of the church as a method of healing, he is immune. When he goes beyond that, puts his spiritual agencies aside and takes up the agencies of the flesh, his immunity ceases. He is then competing with physicians on their own ground, using the same instrumentalities, and arrogating to himself the right to pursue the same methods without the same training.[108]

More recently a New York court upheld the conviction of a Doctor of Divine Metaphysics who held a certificate from the Church of Divine Metaphysics, but who failed to convince the trial and appellate courts that he had been practicing religion in good faith.[109] The court concluded that he held himself out as being able to diagnose and treat disease, injury and deformity, and prescribed drugs, laid on the hands, and used electric vibrators and other gadgets. The court concluded that this person, in assuming to practice the tenets of a church "as a shield to cover a business undertaking," was "a faker and quack who claims the cloak of religion to hide his illegitimate practices."[110] Many other so-called faith healers have been convicted of the crime of the unlawful practice of medicine,[111] particularly where the healer undertakes to diagnose disease, or uses gadgets, or prescribes drugs or diets.[112] In one case, the court took note of the fact that while the accused claimed to be the pastor of a church, it had a negligible membership of only twelve, and the trial court found that this so-called church (named The Christian Church of the Divine Revelation) was merely a front for an office practice.[113] This man not only solicited patronage, for a consideration, but also purported to be able to cure fallen arches. In all of these cases the courts ruled that it was a proper function of the jury to decide, on the evidence, whether prayer was invoked in good faith, or whether the

---

108 Id. at 293, 116 N.E. at 978.
109 People v. Wendel, 68 N.Y.S.2d 267 (Kings Co. Ct. 1946), aff'd, 272 App. Div. 1067, 75 N.Y.S.2d 302 (1947).
110 Id. at 270-71.
111 Fealy v. City of Birmingham, 15 Ala. App. 367, 73 So. 296 (1916); Smith v. People, 51 Colo. 270, 117 Pac. 612 (1911); People v. Handzik, 410 Ill. 295, 102 N.E.2d 340, cert. denied, 343 U.S. 927 (1951); State v. Verbon, 167 Wash. 140, 8 P.2d 1083 (1932).
112 People v. Estep, 346 Ill. App. 132, 104 N.E.2d 562, appeal transferred, 409 Ill. 125, 97 N.E.2d 823 (1952), appeal refused, 413 Ill. 437, 109 N.E.2d 762, cert. denied, 345 U.S. 970 (1953); People v. Blighton, 190 Misc. 569, 75 N.Y.S.2d 194 (Monroe Co. Ct. 1947).
113 People v. Hickey, 157 Misc. 592, 283 N.Y.S. 968 (Sp. Sess. 1935), aff'd, 249 App. Div. 611, 292 N.Y.S. 177 (1936).

healer's use of prayer was only for the purpose of evading the medical practice act of the state. Thus a secular jury in a secular court is inescapably involved in determining whether a man's practice of the tenets of a religion was really in good faith. Of course this cannot be reconciled with an absolutist conception of religious liberty, but the alternative is to permit frauds and quacks to endanger health, and life itself, by practicing medicine without a minimum stock of medical knowledge and skill. Our legal system does not concede that one has a right to practice medicine merely because he asserts that what he is doing is in accordance with the tenets of something described as a religion.

In the important case of *United States v. Ballard*,[114] decided in 1944, the United States Supreme Court came to grips with this problem, and while the Justices were not in agreement, the majority view was consistent with the general tenor of the state faith-healer cases. Guy and Edna Ballard and their son Donald founded and operated a profitable religious cult known as the "I Am." The teachings of the Ballards were represented as having been dictated by St. Germain, a bishop at Auxerre who had died in the year 448. They were brought to trial on a charge of mail fraud in the federal district court for the southern district of California, at which the main issue turned on the claim of the Ballards to possessing great healing powers. Mrs. Ballard testified that her husband had healed 20,000 people in an eight-year period. There was considerable testimony that the Ballards had claimed to be able to cure such incurable diseases as cancer, and such distressing conditions as old age, blindness and misery. Many witnesses testified at the trial in behalf of the accused Ballards. One witness, the mother of seven children, testified that she had been "healed from paralysis, diabetes, an acute heart condition, very serious nervous disorders," pneumonia, neuritis, arthritis, inflammatory rheumatism, and malaria fever. A sardonic prosecutor asked her whether she had ever heard of the word "hypochondria," to which she tartly replied, "I am not a walking dictionary."[115] The Ballards sold all sorts of books and other publications, charts, pictures and phonograph records made of a blue substance which was represented as having some special vitalizing quality.

The government instituted this prosecution on the theory that the Ballards had used the mails to perpetrate frauds. In his closing argument the chief prosecutor summed up by declaring that "crime is no less odious because it is shellacked with a little bit of religion."[116] The intellectual problem of the trial judge, however, was to determine which

---

[114] 322 U.S. 78 (1944). For a full treatment of this case see Fellman, The Limits of Freedom 6-19 (1959); Kurland, Religion and the Law 75-79 (1962).
[115] Transcript, pp. 594-95, United States v. Ballard, 322 U.S. 78 (1944).
[116] Transcript, p. 1496, United States v. Ballard, supra note 115.

question would be the proper question for the jury to decide. Should the jury, for example, be asked to decide whether Guy Ballard had really shaken hands with St. Germain, as had been claimed, or whether Ballard had in fact cured the incurable? Early in the trial the judge adopted the theory that the jury was not to concern itself with the truth or soundness, or even the plausibility, of the "I Am" doctrines. On this theory the judge ruled on the admissibility of evidence and instructed the jury at the end of the trial. He told the jury that the only proper question it could properly decide was whether the defendants honestly and in good faith believed the things they preached. He said that since healing by prayer was as lawful as healing by drugs, the lawfulness of the calling of the religious healer was not in question. While the jury must not pass on the objective truth or falsity of religious beliefs and doctrines, the judge asserted that "even though a person or persons are advocating a religious activity, . . . they must do so in good faith and without making any substantial misrepresentations with the intent to deceive." In short, the verity of the religious beliefs of the defendants was not an issue in a mail fraud case, but the sincerity with which they professed and acted upon these beliefs was.

On appeal from the conviction, the Court of Appeals for the Ninth Circuit reversed the conviction on the ground that the trial judge's distinction between the verity and sincerity of the defendants' beliefs was erroneous.[117] The Supreme Court reversed, holding that the trial judge's theory had been consistent with the requirements of American constitutional law. Counsel for the Ballards argued, without success, that it was "wholly impractical in a country with such a divergency of beliefs as ours," to put on trial either the verity or the sincerity of religious beliefs.[118] Counsel insisted that jurors will almost invariably make a finding of bad faith where they are dealing with religious beliefs which seem to them unbelievable. In other words, it was argued in behalf of the Ballards on the appeal that it would be no less difficult to prove good faith than it would be to establish the truth about the religious doctrines in question.

Speaking for the Court, Justice Douglas took the position that the theory on which the trial judge had conducted the case was required by the constitutional guaranty of religious liberty.[119] It would be highly

---

117 Ballard v. United States, 138 F.2d 540 (9th Cir. 1943).
118 Brief for appellant, p. 32, Ballard v. United States, supra note 115.
119 For earlier mail fraud cases where only the question of good faith was allowed to go to the jury, see United States v. White, 150 Fed. 379 (D. Md. 1906); Post v. United States, 135 Fed. 1 (5th Cir. 1905); New v. United States, 245 Fed. 710 (9th Cir. 1917), cert. denied, 246 U.S. 665 (1918). Cf. School of Magnetic Healing v. McAnnulty, 187 U.S. 94 (1902), a mail fraud case involving a non-religious mental healer. This case was decided on statutory rather than constitutional grounds.

improper, under this guaranty, to permit the jury to decide whether the Ballards' religious doctrines were true or false. The basic freedom of religious thought, said Justice Douglas, "embraces the right to maintain theories of life and of death and of the hereafter which are rank heresy to followers of the orthodox faiths. Heresy trials are foreign to our Constitution. Men may believe what they cannot prove. They may not be put to the proof of their religious doctrines or beliefs. Religious experiences which are as real as life to some may be incomprehensible to others."[120] Justice Douglas went on to point out that "many take their gospel from the New Testament. But it would hardly be supposed that they could be tried before a jury charged with the duty of determining whether those teachings contained false representations. The miracles of the New Testament, the Divinity of Christ, life after death, the power of prayer are deep in the religious convictions of many. If one could be sent to jail because a jury in a hostile environment found those teachings false, little indeed would be left of religious freedom."[121]

Since the authors of the Constitution were fully aware of this country's religious diversity, they fashioned a charter which, in the words of Justice Douglas, permitted "the widest possible toleration of conflicting views. Man's relation to his God was made no concern of the state. He was granted the right to worship as he pleased and to answer to no man for the verity of his religious views."[122] Even though the religious views of the Ballards might seem incredible or even preposterous to most people, Justice Douglas pointed out that if a jury can pass on their truth or falsity, then this can also be done with the beliefs of any religious sect. "When the triers of fact undertake that task," he wrote, "they enter a forbidden domain."[123] In this sense all types of religions are in the same position.

Thus a majority of the Supreme Court concluded that the court of appeals had erred in holding that the question of the truth of the Ballards' religious doctrines should have been submitted to the jury, and remanded the case to the court of appeals for the consideration of other grounds for reversal advanced by the Ballards. Three Justices, speaking through Chief Justice Stone, voted to sustain the conviction, stressing that the issue of the truth of the religious doctrines under consideration had been withheld from the jury. All the jury had been asked to decide was whether the Ballards honestly believed in what they said. "On this issue," said the Chief Justice, "the jury, on ample evidence . . . found a verdict of guilty. The state of one's mind is a fact as capable of fraudulent misrepresentation as is one's physical condition

---

[120] United States v. Ballard, 322 U.S. 78, 86 (1944).
[121] Id. at 87.
[122] Ibid.
[123] Ibid.

or the state of his bodily health."[124] He declared that he was "not pre-
pared to say that the constitutional guaranty of freedom of religion
affords immunity from criminal prosecution for the fraudulent procure-
ment of money by false statements as to one's religious experiences,
more than it renders polygamy or libel immune from criminal prosecution. . . . I cannot say that freedom of thought and worship includes
freedom to procure money by making knowingly false statements about
one's religious experiences."[125]

Finally Justice Jackson also dissented, but on the altogether different
position that this trial should never have been held. Though he saw
nothing in the teachings of the Ballards "but humbug, untainted by any
trace of truth," he took the position, expressed in very strong language,
that no religious beliefs are constitutionally indictable. He did not think
it was possible to "separate an issue as to what is believed from considerations as to what is believable."[126] He thought that the normal test
of whether one believes something to be false is whether it is proved to
be false. In addition, Justice Jackson argued that it was psychologically
impossible for juries to separate fancied from real religious experiences.
He also insisted that such experiences cannot be verified in the minds of
people who lack religious insight. All religions, he declared, "make
enormous assumptions, generally on the basis of revelations authenti-
cated by some sign or miracle."[127] Though the "I Am" doctrine seemed
to be very doubtful to Justice Jackson, he observed that apparently
some people find refreshment and courage in such teachings, and thus
he found it hard to say that they do not get what they pay for. "Scores
of sects flourish in this country," he went on to say, "by teaching what
to me are queer notions. It is plain that there is a wide variety in
American religious taste. The Ballards are not alone in catering to it
with a pretty dubious product."[128] If there had been any wrong in this
case, it was not financial but rather on the spiritual plane, but this is
precisely what the Constitution put beyond the reach of the prosecutor.
Thus Justice Jackson concluded that he favored dismissing the indict-
ment "and have done with this business of judicially examining other
people's faiths."

It is difficult not to concede that there is great merit in the position
taken by Justice Jackson in Ballards' case. Nevertheless, it cannot be
denied that the majority point of view is basically friendly to religious
freedom. All of the Justices agreed that the jury should not be permitted to rule on the objective truth or falsity of religious doctrines,

---

[124] Id. at 89-90.
[125] Id. at 88-89.
[126] Id. at 92.
[127] Id. at 94.
[128] Ibid.

and this is altogether consistent with the spirit of the American constitutional guaranty of religious freedom. All but Justice Jackson agreed that the practice of religion should not serve as a cover for taking money under false pretenses, and the notion that good faith belief can be litigated in a civil court is by no means a novel one in American law, as we noted in reviewing the religious healing cases. Finally, subsequent developments do not suggest that the Ballard decision opened the floodgates of criminal prosecution. It is fitting and proper that this should be so, since it is very difficult to accept the idea that very many jurors will conclude that the defendant honestly believed something which the jurors consider unbelievable. It is also a fair guess that there must be more than a few clergymen, even in the most respectable sects, who do not privately believe that everything they profess is true. They accept offerings of money, as did the Ballards, but we are not in any great hurry to hale them into court to answer to charges of fraud. I think that this is not too stiff a price to pay for the enjoyment of religious liberty.

General Welfare. American courts have had occasion to make the point, in numerous decisions, that religious considerations will not justify violations of laws enacted for the general welfare. Thus, many years ago the Supreme Court of Kentucky upheld the conviction of a revivalist preacher for breach of the peace, as a consequence of his use of obscene and vulgar language in the pulpit, the court noting that "one will not be permitted to commit a breach of the peace, under the guise of preaching the gospel."[129] Nor will the fact that one who commits a breach of the peace on a public street was engaged in selling religious publications bar a conviction.[130] Similarly, the possession and exhibition of obscene literature and pictures cannot be justified on grounds of religious purpose or motive.[131] The Court of Appeals for the Eighth Circuit recently held that trespass upon United States Army property cannot be legally justified because the defendants were motivated to protest against war and the use of nuclear weapons on religious grounds, since it is well established that "the doing of an act motivated by religious belief or thought to be a proper exercise of free speech does not necessarily preclude criminal liability."[132] In the well-known case of *Chaplinsky v. New Hampshire*,[133] decided in 1942, the Supreme Court of the United

---

[129] Delk v. Commonwealth, 166 Ky. 39, 47, 178 S.W. 1129, 1132 (1915).

[130] People v. Hussock, 6 Misc. 2d 182, 23 N.Y.S.2d 520 (Sp. Sess. 1940), cert. denied, 312 U.S. 659 (1941). The court said "It must be said . . . that most rights under the law are relative and must be exercised with reference to the public weal." Id. at 184, 23 N.Y.S.2d at 522.

[131] State v. Kowan, 156 N.E.2d 170 (Ohio C.P. 1958).

[132] Holdridge v. United States, 282 F.2d 302, 311 (8th Cir. 1960). A conviction of a Jehovah's Witness for violation of a state anti-subversion law was set aside in Taylor v. Mississippi, 319 U.S. 583 (1943).

[133] 315 U.S. 568 (1942). For similar rulings see Oney v. Oklahoma City, 120

States affirmed the conviction of a Jehovah's Witness who had cursed the town marshall on a public street in violation of a statute. The strongly libertarian Justice Frank Murphy, who spoke for a unanimous Court, asserted that he could not "conceive that cursing a public officer is the exercise of religion in any sense of the term."[134] He noted that the prevention and punishment of "certain well-defined and narrowly limited classes of speech" have never been thought to raise constitutional issues. "These include the lewd and obscene, the profane, the libelous, and the insulting or 'fighting' words—those which by their very utterance inflict injury or tend to incite an immediate breach of the peace." Such utterances are not an "essential part of any exposition of ideas, and are of such slight social values as a step to truth that any benefit that may be derived from them is clearly outweighed by the social interest in order and morality."[135]

It is always hazardous for anyone to undertake to violate on religious grounds laws adopted to promote or protect the general welfare. During the Prohibition era, violators of the National Prohibition Act and of the regulations issued under the act were not immune from prosecution because their actions were grounded in religious practices.[136] More recently, the Court of Appeals for the Third Circuit affirmed an action brought against a farmer by the United States to collect civil penalties under the Agricultural Adjustment Act of 1938 for marketing wheat in excess of the stipulated quota.[137] The farmer's defense was that he regarded it to be his religious duty to produce as much food as he could, and thus the law was unconstitutional as an interference with his religious freedom. Judge Maris said that the first amendment "does not include freedom from all regulation of an individual's acts and conduct as contradistinguished from his beliefs. On the contrary, the enforcement of a reasonable nondiscriminatory regulation of conduct by governmental authority to preserve peace, tranquillity and a sound economic order does not violate the First Amendment merely because it may inhibit conduct on the part of individuals which is sincerely claimed by them to be religiously motivated."[138]

F.2d 861 (10 Cir. 1941); Bevins v. Prindable, 39 F. Supp. 708 (E.D. Ill. 1941), aff'd, 314 U.S. 573 (1941).

[134] Chaplinsky v. New Hampshire, 315 U.S. 568, 571 (1942). The Legislature of Maryland adopted a statute on April 21, 1649, which imposed a penalty of a ten-shilling fine or a public whipping upon anyone who shall call any person in the colony "an heritick, Scismatick, Idolator, puritan, Independant, Prespiterian popish prest, Jesuite, Jesuited papist, Lutheran, Calvenist, Anabaptist, Brownist, Antinomian, Barrowist, Roundhead, Se'patist, or any other name or terme in a reproachful manner relating to matter of Religion. . . ." 1 Archives of Maryland 245.

[135] 315 U.S. at 572.

[136] Shapiro v. Lyle, 30 F.2d 971 (W.D. Wash. 1929).

[137] United States v. Kissinger, 250 F.2d 940 (3d Cir. 1958).

[138] Id. at 943. Cf. Mitchell v. Pilgrim Holiness Church, 210 F.2d 879 (7th

A long series of cases, most of them involving members of the Jehovah's Witnesses sect, have tested their right to communicate their views in various public places. In the leading case of *Cantwell v. Connecticut*,[139] decided in 1940, a unanimous Supreme Court held a state statute invalid which provided that no person may solicit money for any religious charitable or philanthropic cause, unless upon application the secretary of the public welfare council shall first determine whether the cause is truly a religious one or is a bona fide object of charity or philanthropy and conforms to reasonable standards of efficiency and integrity. The Court ruled that this amounted to an unconstitutional censorship of religion. At the same time it pointed out that this does not mean that people are free, under the cloak of religion, to commit frauds upon the public, for which penal laws are available. Similarly, the Supreme Court has held unconstitutional as a forbidden tax on religion the imposition by local governments of license taxes upon Jehovah's Witnesses for the privilege of door-to-door or street solicitation. In the basic decision on this subject, the Court noted that the hand distribution of religious tracts is an age-old and potent form of missionary evangelism which is entitled to the same legal status that is accorded to worship and preaching from pulpits.[140] The fact that the religious literature is sold by itinerant preachers does not transform evangelism into a commercial enterprise. The Court has also ruled that Jehovah's Witnesses may not be restrained from holding meetings in public parks through the operation of discriminatory local ordinances.[141] The right of members of this sect to distribute handbills on the streets or other public places,[142] and to ring door bells in the course of their religious activities,[143] has been sustained repeatedly, though reasonable regulations designed to prevent avoidable annoyance and disturbance

---

Cir. 1954), which held that a religious group operating a printing plant is obliged to comply with the Fair Labor Standards Act.

[139] 310 U.S. 296 (1940).

[140] Murdock v. Pennsylvania, 319 U.S. 105 (1943), overruling Jones v. Opelika, 316 U.S. 584 (1942), judgment vacated, 319 U.S. 103 (1943). The same point was made in Busey v. District of Columbia, 319 U.S. 579 (1943), and in Follett v. Town of McCormick, 321 U.S. 573 (1944), where Justice Douglas said: "Freedom of religion is not merely reserved for those with a long purse. Preachers of the more orthodox faiths are not engaged in commercial undertakings because they are dependent on their calling for a living." 321 U.S. at 576. See also City of Blue Island v. Kozul, 379 Ill. 511, 41 N.E.2d 515 (1942), reprinted in 8 John Marshall L.Q. 25 (1942), and the article by the judge who wrote this opinion, Miner, Religion and the Law, 21 Chi.-Kent L. Rev. 156 (1943).

[141] Fowler v. Rhode Island, 345 U.S. 67 (1953); Niemotko v. Maryland, 340 U.S. 268 (1951).

[142] Largent v. Texas, 318 U.S. 418 (1943); Jamison v. Texas, 318 U.S. 413 (1943); Lovell v. City of Griffin, 303 U.S. 444 (1938); Schneider v. Irvington, 308 U.S. 147 (1939).

[143] Martin v. City of Struthers, 319 U.S. 141 (1943); People v. Dale, 47 N.Y.S.2d 702 (City Ct. 1944).

of the peace of others have been sustained.[144] The Supreme Court has also ruled that the Jehovah's Witnesses may not be denied access to the streets of a company-owned town,[145] or to those of a town owned entirely by the United States.[146] In addition, it has been held that the use by members of this sect of loudspeaker equipment cannot be made to depend upon the unfettered judgment of some administrative official,[147] though reasonable regulation of the use of loud-speakers has been affirmed.[148] Finally, in the leading case of *Cox v. New Hampshire*,[149] the Supreme Court ruled that a city may lawfully require Jehovah's Witnesses, or any other group, to secure a special license before holding a parade or procession on the streets. Chief Justice Hughes stressed the fact that the regulation of the use of the streets, to assure public safety and convenience in their use, is a traditional exercise of control by local government. It was carefully noted that as construed by the state courts, the statute in question did not vest an unfettered discretion in the hands of the administrative authorities concerned with its application.

Whether one may lawfully refuse to serve on a jury for religious reasons has been litigated, but not very extensively. A federal district judge in the State of Washington ruled in 1943 that the refusal of a Jehovah's Witness to serve as a juror is justified by the first amendment guaranty of the free exercise of religion.[150] On the other hand, the highest court of Minnesota ruled the other way in 1963, holding that the right to religious freedom "is not an absolute, unfettered privilege," and that the fundamental duty of the citizen to serve on a jury does not interfere with that freedom.[151] The burden on religious conviction, if any, is too slight to serve as a proper excuse for not serving. The court feared that a contrary holding would "invite the erosion of every other obligation a citizen owes his community and his country."[152]

---

144 People v. Vaughan, 65 Cal. App. 2d 844, 150 P.2d 964 (Super. Ct. 1944); Watchtower Bible & Tract Soc'y v. Metropolitan Life Ins. Co., 297 N.Y. 339, 79 N.E.2d 433 (1948), cert. denied, 335 U.S. 886 (1948). An ordinance which merely required any seller of magazines, books or other articles on the streets to secure an identification badge from a local official was upheld over objections by several Jehovah's Witnesses in City of Manchester v. Leiby, 117 F.2d 661 (1st Cir. 1941), cert. denied, 313 U.S. 562 (1941). The court held that this did not constitute any censorship of religion, and imposed no substantial burden upon the free exercise of religion.
145 Marsh v. Alabama, 326 U.S. 501 (1946).
146 Tucker v. Texas, 326 U.S. 517 (1946).
147 Saia v. New York, 334 U.S. 558 (1948); State v. Corbisiero, 170 A.2d 74 (N.J. County Ct. 1961).
148 Kovacs v. Cooper, 336 U.S. 77 (1949).
149 312 U.S. 569 (1941). In Frazee's Case, 63 Mich. 396, 30 N.W. 72 (1886), an ordinance which left the granting of street parade licenses to the unregulated discretion of the officials was held invalid.
150 United States v. Hillyard, 52 F. Supp. 612 (E.D. Wash. 1943).
151 In re Jenison, 120 N.W.2d 515, 517 (Minn. 1963).
152 Id. at 518.

The United States Supreme Court granted certiorari in this case,[153] but remanded it to the Minnesota court for reconsideration in the light of a recent decision dealing with the denial of unemployment compensation where unavailability for work rested on religious grounds.[154] On remand, the Minnesota court got the message and reversed itself.

Finally, in the general area of public welfare regulation, a unanimous court made an important decision in 1961, in *Torcaso v. Watkins.*[155] Torcaso had been appointed to the office of notary public, but he was refused a commission to serve because he would not declare his belief in God. Article 37 of the declaration of rights of the Maryland constitution provided that such a declaration may be required as a qualification for holding office. The Court ruled that this was undoubtedly a religious test, which the federal government is specifically forbidden to impose by the Constitution,[156] and which is abhorrent to our tradition. Thus it is forbidden to the states by the due process clause of the fourteenth amendment. Neither the federal government nor any state may lawfully force a person to profess either a belief or a disbelief in any religion. It is immaterial that no one is compelled to hold public office, since this does not warrant the imposition of criteria forbidden by the Constitution.[157]

Sunday Laws. Sunday closing laws date from the very beginning of the colonial settlements,[158] and were almost universally upheld in early state supreme court decisions.[159] Today all states but Alaska have laws of some sort which forbid on Sunday, activity which is otherwise permissible. Writing in 1904, in his influential treatise on the police power, Professor Ernst Freund declared that "the protection of Sunday as a day of rest has a clear relation to public order and comfort," and that "it is well established that the character of Sunday legislation is secular and not religious. . . . The enforced abstention from work has been

---

[153] In re Jenison, 375 U.S. 14 (1963).
[154] Sherbert v. Verner, 374 U.S. 398 (1963).
[155] 367 U.S. 488 (1961).
[156] U.S. Const. art VI.
[157] Some courts have held that it is not improper to ask a witness in court about his religious beliefs as they relate to issues of competency and credibility. See Commonwealth ex rel. Graeser v. Myers, 189 Pa. Super. 198, 150 A.2d 380 (1959); Levy v. Hayward, 248 F.2d 152 (App. D.C. 1957). The latter case involved a suit for damages for alleged denial of first amendment rights because such questions were asked. The court ruled that the plaintiff had failed to state a claim on which relief could be granted. See Duffie, The Requirement of a Religious Belief for Competency of a Witness, 11 S.C.L.Q. 548 (1959).
[158] See Note, 73 Harv. L. Rev. 729 (1960); Johnson & Yost, Separation of Church and State in the United States ch. 19-20 (Rev. ed. 1948); Pfeffer, Church, State and Freedom 227-41 (1953).
[159] See People v. Ruggles, 8 Johnson R. 290 (N.Y. 1811); Davis v. Fish, 1 Greene 406 (Iowa 1848); Brimhall v. Van Campen, 8 Minn. 1 (1858); Kountz v. Price, 40 Miss. 341 (1866); Karwisch v. The Mayor & Council, 44 Ga. 205 (1871); Davis v. Sommerville, 128 Mass. 594 (1880).

34

held to be justified by the experience, that periods of rest from ordinary pursuits are requisite to the moral and physical well-being of the people."[160] As Freund suggested, the legal case for upholding Sunday laws shifted from religious to secular police power considerations, such as the preservation of good morals and the peace and good order of society.[161] In several cases decided before the due process clause of the fourteenth amendment was permitted to assume any real significance— and this process dates only from 1925—the Supreme Court upheld the validity of Sunday closing laws as against various legal objections.[162] In our day, state appellate courts generally sustain such laws as being secular in character and as embodying proper police power objectives.[163] It is also denied that these laws interfere with anyone's freedom of religion. Thus an Ohio judge recently wrote: "It is difficult—we think impossible—to make even a convincing argument that such a law has any relation whatsoever to religion, that is, that it has anything to do with man's relation to his God. It requires nothing. It imposes nothing. It dictates nothing. It leaves him completely free to choose his religion and practice it without let or hindrance."[164]

The present position of the Supreme Court on the question of the constitutionality of Sunday closing laws was spelled out in four important cases decided in May, 1961.[165] In two of these cases, discount department stores challenged the validity of the Sunday closing laws

---

[160] Freund, The Police Power 168-69 (1904).

[161] See, e.g., City of Mt. Vernon v. Julian, 369 Ill. 447, 17 N.E.2d 52 (1938); People v. C. Klinck Packing Co., 214 N.Y. 121, 108 N.E. 278 (1915); State v. Powell, 58 Ohio St. 324, 50 N.E. 900 (1898). There have been a few decisions the other way. A Sunday closing law was declared unconstitutional in Ex parte Newman, 9 Cal. 502 (1858), but this decision was overruled in Ex parte Andrews, 18 Cal. 678 (1861). Pacesetter Homes, Inc. v. Village of South Holland, 18 Ill. 2d 247, 163 N.E.2d 464 (1959), held an ordinance invalid which forbade all business activity on Sunday except for "emergency" needs. The court said that since there is nothing in mere business activity which disturbs others in their Sunday worship, the ordinance went beyond police power purposes to promote religious worship, which is not a proper governmental function. A county judge in Ohio recently ruled that Sunday closing laws were unconstitutional since their purpose is to support the religious and devotional life of the community. State v. Woodville Appliance, Inc., 171 N.E.2d 565 (Ohio County Ct. 1960).

[162] Petit v. Minnesota, 177 U.S. 164 (1900); Hennington v. Georgia, 163 U.S. 299 (1896); Soon Hing v. Crowley, 113 U.S. 703 (1885).

[163] The cases are legion. A few recent cases are: Kentucky v. Arlan's Dep't Store, 357 S.W.2d 708 (Ky. 1962), appeal dismissed, 371 U.S. 218 (1962); State v. Fass, 62 N.J. Super. 265, 162 A.2d 608 (1960); People v. Friedman, 302 N.Y. 75, 96 N.E.2d 184 (1950); Ohio v. Broughton, 171 Ohio St. 261, 168 N.E.2d 744 (1960), appeal dismissed and cert. denied, 367 U.S. 905 (1961); State v. Kidd, 167 Ohio St. 521, 150 N.E.2d 413 (1958); Commonwealth v. Bander, 188 Pa. Super. 424, 145 A.2d 915 (1958); Carolina Amusement Co. v. Martin, 236 S.C. 558, 115 S.E.2d 273 (1960).

[164] State v. Ullner, 105 Ohio App. 546, 549, 143 N.E.2d 849, 851 (1957).

[165] McGowan v. Maryland, 366 U.S. 420 (1961); Gallagher v. Crown Kosher Super Market, 366 U.S. 617 (1961); Two Guys from Harrison-Allentown, Inc. v. McGinley, 366 U.S. 582 (1961); Braunfeld v. Brown, 366 U.S. 599 (1961).

of Maryland[166] and Pennsylvania.[167] Aside from the equal protection issue, arising from the existence of exemptions in the statutes, which was settled in favor of allowing legislatures a wide discretion in making classifications, the Court disposed of the religious liberty issue by holding that commercial establishments have no standing to raise it, since they alleged only economic injury, the record being silent as to religious beliefs. In addition, eight Justices agreed that the Sunday laws did not violate the principle of the separation of church and state. Chief Justice Warren said that while it is indisputable that the original Sunday laws were motivated by religious considerations, they have evolved into temporal statutes, and are now part of a large body of secular legislation dealing with public health and safety. These laws promote a day of rest for all, and thus to bar Sunday would be an act of hostility towards the public welfare. He stressed the fact that the Maryland Supreme Court had found that the statutory purpose was not to aid religion but to set aside a day for rest and recreation.[168] The establishment clause of the first amendment, the Chief Justice declared, does not ban legislation which merely happens to coincide or harmonize with the tenets of some or all religions. He noted, for example, that the laws dealing with murder, polygamy and adultery coincide with religious teaching. He added that the state was trying to do more than assure that everyone rests one day in seven; it had in mind rest, repose, recreation, tranquility, visiting back and forth, and it cannot be said that any day would accomplish this purpose. It is also common knowledge, he said, that Sunday has come to have special significance as a rest day in this country. In a lengthy concurring opinion, Justice Frankfurter stressed that the legislative finding that there is no alternative to Sunday as a day of rest is not unreasonable; the day is more convenient, Sunday laws are easier to enforce, it has a better community atmosphere, most people prefer it that way, and all courts agree. Justice Douglas dissented alone, maintaining that in origin and purpose Sunday laws serve and satisfy the religious predispositions of our Christian communities, and that in adopting them the government abandons its neutrality in religious matters. He insisted that a law requiring one day of rest each week was quite different from a law designating Sunday as the day.

The other two cases, however, involved suits brought by Orthodox Jews whose religion required them to close their business establishments on Saturday, and while the Court upheld the challenged laws, the Justices were divided six to three.[169] Speaking for the Court, Chief

---

[166] McGowan v. Maryland, 366 U.S. 420 (1961).
[167] Two Guys from Harrison-Allentown, Inc. v. McGinley, 366 U.S. 582 (1961).
[168] McGowan v. State, 220 Md. 117, 115 A.2d 156 (1959).
[169] Gallagher v. Crown Kosher Super Market, 366 U.S 617 (1961); Braunfeld

Justice Warren pointed out[170] that the statute did not make criminal the holding of any religious belief or opinion, and that it did not force anyone to embrace a religious belief or to say or believe anything in conflict with his religious tenets. "However," he declared, "the freedom to act, even when the action is in accord with one's religious convictions, is not totally free from legislative restrictions."[171] He pointed out that the statute did not make any religious practice unlawful, but merely regulated a secular activity. In fact, he also noted that it did not inconvenience all Jews, but only those who believe that it is necessary to work on Sunday, and even the Orthodox Jews were not faced with such serious choices as forsaking their religion or subjecting themselves to criminal prosecutions. At most, the Chief Justice thought that the burden on the complaining parties was indirect. He said that we are a cosmopolitan nation with almost 300 religions, and that it cannot be expected that the legislature will enact no law regulating conduct which may in some way result in an economic disadvantage to some sects and not to others. Invidious discrimination between religions is constitutionally invalid, said the Chief Justice, "but if the State regulates conduct by enacting a general law within its power, the purpose and effect of which is to advance the State's secular goals, the statute is valid despite its indirect burden on religious observance unless the State may accomplish its purpose by means which do not impose such a burden."[172] The Court could find no alternative to setting aside Sunday as the best day for rest, repose, tranquility, recreation, and the like. Of course, Chief Justice Warren pointed out, the state is free to create an exemption for such people as the complaining parties, but it is not constitutionally required to do so, since it has a right to believe that such exemptions would undermine the state's goal and add to its enforcement problems. Furthermore, an exemption might give an economic advantage to those who open on Sunday over their competitors, it might require state inquiry into the religious sincerity of the individual claiming exemption, and it might lead to religious discrimination by employers in hiring workers. In his separate concurring opinion, Justice Frankfurter argued that the community interest in a day of repose overbalanced the economic disadvantage to the enterpriser, especially since this is the only feasible way of achieving the desired goal.

Justice Stewart dissented because he thought that in compelling the Orthodox Jew to choose between his religious faith and his economic

---

v. Brown, 366 U.S. 599 (1961). These cases came up from Massachusetts and Pennsylvania respectively.
[170] The main arguments were made in the case of Braunfeld v. Brown, 366 U.S. 599 (1961).
[171] Id. at 603.
[172] Id. at 607.

survival, he was confronted with a "cruel choice."[173] He went on to say: "It is a choice which I think no State can constitutionally demand. For me this is not something that can be swept under the rug and forgotten in the interest of enforced Sunday togetherness." For Justice Brennan, a law which requires an individual to choose between his business and his religion prohibits the free exercise of religion. The only state interest he could find was the mere convenience of having everyone rest on the same day, and he thought that this was not sufficiently substantial to outweigh a claim to religious freedom, which has such an honored place in our constitutional hierarchy. In his dissent Justice Douglas stressed that the label which a state attaches to a law involving constitutional questions is not binding upon the Supreme Court, and he could find here no room for balancing one interest against another.[174]

The Court took this occasion to review the whole Sunday closing law problem in very great detail; the opinions cover 196 pages in the official reports. Clearly this was a major test of an ancient legal problem, and clearly a majority of the Court does not find in them any invalid restraint upon the freedom of religion, even for people whose religion requires that some other day serve as a day of rest, nor any impermissible establishment of religion.

An interesting variation of this problem was involved in *Sherbert v. Verner*,[175] decided in 1963, in which the Supreme Court was concerned with the plight of a textile mill operator in South Carolina who, as a member of the Seventh-Day Adventist Church, was discharged by her employer because she would not work on Saturday, and was unable to get another job because of her conscientious scruples against working on her Sabbath. Her claim under the South Carolina Unemployment Compensation Act was denied by the state commission, on the ground that to be eligible for benefits, a claimant must, in the words of the statute, be "able to work" and be "available for work." One is not eligible, the commission held, if he has failed to accept available and suitable work "without good cause." The United States Supreme Court ruled that this construction of the statute constituted a "governmental regulation of religious *beliefs* as such. . . . Government may neither compel affirmation of a repugnant belief . . . ; nor penalize or discriminate against individuals or groups because they hold religious views abhorrent to the authorities. . . ."[176] The Court took the position that the state's disqualification of the claimant was unmistakably a type of pres-

---

173 Id. at 616.
174 McGowan v. Maryland, 366 U.S. 420, 575-76 (1961).
175 374 U.S. 398 (1963).
176 Id. at 402.

sure upon her to forego her practice of her religion, since she was in effect compelled to choose between following the precepts of her religion and forfeiting benefits, on the one hand, and abandoning a religious precept in order to accept work, on the other hand. Furthermore, the Court said that it did not matter whether unemployment compensation benefits are called a "right" or a "privilege," since in either event the liberty of religion may not be infringed or denied by imposing conditions. Finally, the Court was unable to identify any compelling state interest which would justify this substantial infringement of first amendment rights. The recent decision[177] upholding the validity of Sunday closing laws was distinguished on the ground that that case dealt with a strong state interest in providing one uniform day of rest for all workers.

Justice Stewart wrote a concurring opinion to make the point that he could not reconcile this decision with the Court's decision in the case involving the application of Sunday closing laws to Orthodox Jews, where, he maintained, the burden was, if anything, greater than here. Justice Harlan filed a dissenting opinion with which Justice White registered his agreement. He maintained that it was the policy of South Carolina to deny compensation where unemployment is due to any personal reasons, however compelling, and that it is therefore wholly irrelevant that the reason is religious conviction. Thus Sherbert was not discriminated against because of her religious beliefs, but because she was not available for work for personal reasons. Justice Harlan also argued that this decision was inconsistent with the Sunday closing case, where the burden on the complaining party was even greater. In Sherbert's case he thought the effect upon her religion was "indirect, remote, and insubstantial."[178]

A case decided by a California District Court of Appeals in 1956[179] offers an interesting contrast with the *Sherbert* case. In this instance, after receiving injuries on the job, the employee refused on religious grounds to accept a blood transfusion. The Industrial Commission denied compensation to the widow on the basis of a finding that her

---

[177] Braunfeld v. Brown, 366 U.S. 599 (1961).

[178] 374 U.S. at 423. It is interesting to note that state courts have usually granted unemployment compensation to persons unable to find suitable work solely because of a religious prohibition against Saturday work. See In re Miller, 243 N.C. 509, 91 S.E.2d 24 (1956); Swenson v. Michigan Employment Security Comm., 340 Mich. 430, 65 N.W.2d 709 (1954); Tary v. Board of Review, 161 Ohio St. 251, 119 N.E.2d 56 (1954); Heisler v. Board of Review, Bureau of Unemployment Compensation, 156 Ohio St. 395, 102 N.E.2d 601 (1951), appeal dismissed, 343 U.S. 939 (1952). Justice Brennan pointed out that of the 28 states that have administrative rulings on the subject under discussion, 22 have held people like Sherbert entitled to benefits. 374 U.S. at 408.

[179] Martin v. Industrial Acc. Comm'n, 147 Cal. App. 2d 137, 304 P.2d 828 (Dist. Ct. App. 1956).

husband died because of an unreasonable refusal to accept, as required by the statute, proper medical treatment. The court said that the decedent had been free to worship and believe as he pleased, but that freedom of religion does not give the worker a right to impose a liability upon his employer when his death results from voluntary practice of his religion.

Child Welfare. The community's interest in the welfare of children often collides with claims to the exercise of religious freedom, and when this happens the courts must make choices. A leading example of a case where the decision went in favor of child welfare was *Prince v. Massachusetts*,[180] decided by the Supreme Court in 1944. A Jehovah's Witness who was the aunt and custodian of a nine-year old girl was convicted of violating the Massachusetts child labor laws by permitting the child to sell publications of their sect on the streets. Both Mrs. Prince and the girl testified that they were ordained ministers, and that they regarded their challenged activity to be a religious duty. The Justices, dividing five to four, upheld the conviction. Justice Rutledge pointed out that "the family itself is not beyond regulation in the public interest, as against a claim of religious liberty," and that, as *parens patriae*, the state's authority to safeguard the general interest in the well-being of children "is not nullified merely because the parent grounds his claim to control the child's course of conduct on religion or conscience."[181] Especially in respect to public activities and matters of employment, Justice Rutledge asserted, the authority of the state over children's activities is broader than over similar actions of adults, because "a democratic society rests, for its continuance, upon the healthy, well-rounded growth of young people into full maturity as citizens. . . ."[182] Thus the state may protect society from such evils as the "crippling effects of child employment," particularly in public places. In addition to the ordinary hazards which even adults face on the public streets, the Court alluded to such dangers to children as may result from "emotional excitement" and "psychological or physical injury." And Justice Rutledge went on to observe that "parents may be free to become martyrs themselves. But it does not follow they are free, in identical circumstances, to make martyrs of their children before they have reached the age of full and legal discretion when they can make that choice for themselves."[183]

In his dissenting opinion, Justice Murphy argued that the girl had been engaged in a genuine religious activity which to her was a form of

---

[180] 321 U.S. 158 (1944).
[181] Id. at 166.
[182] Id. at 168.
[183] Id. at 170.

missionary evangelism. Furthermore, he felt that the state had failed completely to show the existence of "any grave or immediate danger to any interest which it may lawfully protect."[184] He said that "the sidewalk, no less than the cathedral or the evangelist's tent, is a proper place, under the Constitution, for the orderly worship of God."[185] In fact, Justice Murphy thought that children who are engaged in religious activity, in groups subject to adult control, are in less danger of harm and vice than other children. In a second dissenting opinion, Justice Jackson maintained that since the Court had previously, though in his judgment mistakenly, decided that the sort of activity in question was evangelism and not commercial enterprise,[186] precedent supported a reversal of the conviction. Nevertheless, speaking also for Justices Roberts and Frankfurter, Justice Jackson expressed the view that all money-raising activities on a public scale are Caesar's affairs, and thus subject to nondiscriminatory regulation by the state.[187] Thus the Court was not actually divided as closely as the five to four division would seem to indicate. If this had been an original proposition, to be disposed of without the guidance of precedent, the Justices would have sustained the conviction of Mrs. Prince by a vote of eight to one.

American courts recognize that parents have very extensive rights to make decisions regarding the health and welfare of their children, and will sustain those rights even in extreme cases that touch the heart.[188] Nevertheless, even where the decisions of the parents are based upon religious convictions, there are many situations where the state may lawfully interfere. Thus, several state courts have ruled, in recent years, that where parents refuse on religious grounds to permit blood transfusions for blue babies born with an RH blood condition, the state may treat the babies as "neglected children," and appoint guardians

---

[184] Id. at 174.
[185] Ibid.
[186] Murdock v. Pennsylvania, 319 U.S. 105 (1943).
[187] The position taken by the Supreme Court in Prince v. Massachusetts, 321 U.S. 158 (1944), was followed in City of Portland v. Thornton, 174 Ore. 508, 149 P.2d 972 (1944). In State v. Richardson, 72 N.H. 178, 27 A.2d 94 (1942), the court held that such activities could not be classified as "business enterprise" or "work" within the meaning of a child labor law.
[188] For an extreme case, see In re Hudson, 13 Wash. 2d 673, 126 P.2d 765 (1942). Here the child was born with a congenital deformity, an abnormally large left arm, which grew into an enormous monstrosity. Doctors recommended amputation as imperatively necessary, but the parents refused, though not on religious grounds. The court was unwilling to interfere with what it regarded as the sacred rights of parents to decide upon the need for a surgical operation upon their child. Cf. In re Seiferth, 127 N.Y.S.2d 63 (Child. Ct. 1954), aff'd, 309 N.Y. 80, 127 N.E.2d 820 (1955), where the court ruled that a twelve-year old boy could be allowed to decide for himself, without parental interference, whether he should undergo an operation for congenital harelip and cleft palate. The court held that it had the power to interfere not only in matters involving life, health and physical welfare, but also to protect the psychological and emotional well-being of the child. Cf. Oakey v. Jackson, (1914) 1 K.B. 216.

for them who may then give their consent to the necessary blood transfusions.[189] The New Jersey court said, in 1962, that while the right of parents to take care of their children is entitled to the highest respect, it is not unlimited, and the interests of society may be paramount. Nor are the sincerity and affection of the parents controlling facts. It conceded that medical science and surgery are not yet exact sciences, and that the result of any given treatment cannot be predicted with complete accuracy, but it insisted that "courts can be guided only by the prevailing medical opinion."[190]

In addition, many state courts have ruled that parents may be punished criminally for refusing on religious grounds to give their children needed medical care, since parents have a legal duty to look after the health of their children, and the failure to do so is a public wrong.[191] In these instances the courts have rejected such defenses as belief in prayer or divine healing, or rejection of medical science and physicians for religious reasons.[192] Similarly, the Utah court, a few years ago, ruled that eight children of a polygamous marriage were "neglected," and made them wards of the juvenile court, on a finding that a polygamous home is an immoral place unfit for children.[193] The court said: "The good name of this State and its people, committed to sustaining a high moral standard, must not be obliged to suffer because of the unsavory social life of appellants and others claiming the constitutional right under the guise of religious freedom to bring shame and embar-

---

[189] State v. Perricone, 37 N.J. 463, 181 A.2d 751 (1962), noted in 12 De Paul L. Rev. 342 (1963), 34 Miss. L.J. 219 (1963), 24 U. Pitt. L. Rev. 624 (1963), 8 Vill. L. Rev. 114 (1962); People ex rel. Wallace v. Labrenz, 411 Ill. 618, 104 N.E.2d 769 (1952), cert. denied, 344 U.S. 824 (1952); Morrison v. State, 252 S.W.2d 97 (Mo. Ct. App. 1952). See Archibald, Medical Aid for Children without Parental Consent, 13 Wyo. L.J. 88 (1958).
[190] State v. Perricone, 37 N.J. 463, 479, 181 A.2d 751, 760 (1962).
[191] See State v. Chenoweth, 163 Ind. 94, 71 N.E. 197 (1904); People v. Pierson, 176 N.Y. 201, 68 N.E. 243 (1903); Beck v. State, 29 Okla. Crim. 240, 233 Pac. 495 (1925); Owens v. State, 6 Okla. Crim. 110, 116 Pac. 345 (1911); Commonwealth v. Breth, 44 Pa. Co. Ct. 56 (1915); Commonwealth v. Hoffman, 29 Pa. Co. Ct. 65 (1903); Mitchell v. Davis, 205 S.W.2d 812 (Tex. Civ. App. 1947). The English courts have taken the position, on common law principles, that a parent who neglects to give his child necessary medical aid, thereby causing death, is guilty of manslaughter, and that a religious belief is not an adequate defense. Rex v. Brooks (1902), 22 C.L.T. 105, 9 B.C.R. 13; The Queen v. Senior (1899) 1 Q.B. 283; The Queen v. Downes (1875) 1 Q.B. 25. In Craig v. Maryland, 220 Md. 590, 155 A.2d 684 (1959), noted in 9 De Paul L. Rev. 271 (1960), the principle was accepted, but the court ruled that the evidence did not establish the necessary "gross and criminal negligence" on the part of the parents.
[192] See Baldwin, Religious Liberty versus Compulsory Medical Attention, 22 Ga. B.J. 558 (1960); Cawley, Criminal Liability in Faith Healing, 39 Minn. L. Rev. 48 (1954); Larson, Child Neglect in the Exercise of Religious Freedom, 32 Chi.-Kent L. Rev. 283 (1954); Trescher & O'Neill, Medical Care for Dependent Children: Manslaughter Liability of the Christian Scientist, 109 U. Penn. L. Rev. 203 (1960).
[193] In re Black, 3 Utah 2d 315, 283 P.2d 887 (1955), cert. denied, 350 U.S. 923 (1955).

rassment to the people in this state."[194] Furthermore, again in the best interests of the child, the courts have repeatedly sustained compulsory school laws over religious objections, holding that parents may be obliged, subject to criminal penalties, to have their children attend either a public or duly qualified private school or to have them taught by qualified private tutors.[195]

IV

It is deceptively easy to misconstrue the statement that our constitutional law is committed to freedom of religion, because in actual fact a claim to religious freedom, under some circumstances, must and should yield to some other more compelling consideration. It is wholly unsupportable to assert that anything to which a religious tag is attached is necessarily lawful. Our legal history bristles with examples which indicate that like all other freedoms, freedom of religion is not and cannot be absolute. This is equally true for the other side of the coin, our commitment to the separation of church and state. It is true that the federal constitutional provision on this subject speaks only of the prohibition of "an establishment of religion" by Congress,[196] but most of the state constitutions go into the matter in greater detail. Thus the declaration of rights of the constitution of Wisconsin, in addition to forbidding any infringement of the right to worship God according to the dictates of conscience, also states that no man shall "be compelled to attend, erect or support any place of worship, or to maintain any ministry, against his consent," and further, that no "preference" shall "be given by law to any religious establishments or modes of worship; nor shall any money be drawn from the treasury for the benefit of religious societies, or religious or theological seminaries."[197] Religious tests as a qualification for any public office or for witnesses in any court are also prohibited,[198] and "sectarian instruction" in the public schools and in

---

[194] Id. at 348, 283 P.2d at 910.
[195] Commonwealth v. Renfrew, 332 Mass. 492, 126 N.E.2d 109 (1955) ; People v. Donner, 302 N.Y. 857, 100 N.E.2d 48 (1951), appeal dismissed, 342 U.S. 884 (1951) ; Commonwealth v. Smoker, 177 Pa. Super. 435, 110 A.2d 740 (1955) ; State v. Hershberger, 150 N.E.2d 671 (Ohio Juv. Ct. 1958), rev'd on other grounds, 168 N.E.2d 12 (Ohio Ct. App. 1959) ; Commonwealth v. Beiler, 168 Pa. Super. 462, 79 A.2d 134 (1951) ; Commonwealth v. Bey, 166 Pa. Super. 136, 70 A.2d 693 (1950), noted in 2 Ala. L. Rev. 320 (1950), 98 U. Pa. L. Rev. 923 (1950) ; Rice v. Commonwealth, 188 Va. 224, 49 S.E.2d 342 (1948) ; State ex rel. Shoreline School Dist. v. Superior Court, 155 Wash. 175, 346 P.2d 999 (1959), noted in 35 Wash. L. Rev. 151 (1960) ; cf. People v. Levisen, 404 Ill. 574, 90 N.E.2d 213 (1950), and Wright v. State, 21 Okla. Crim. 430, 209 Pac. 179 (1922), where home instruction was found to satisfy the school law. The right to attend an Amish school was upheld in State ex rel. Chalfin v. Glick, 172 Ohio St. 249, 175 N.E.2d 68 (1961). See Haight, The Amish School Controversy, 31 Ohio B.J. 846 (1958).
[196] U.S. Const. amend. I.
[197] Wisc. Const. art. I, § 18.
[198] Wisc. Const. art. I, § 19.

the state university is forbidden.[199] It has become customary to lump all of these ideas together as the concept of the separation of church and state. Thomas Jefferson once referred to the "wall of separation" which our constitutional law has erected between state and church,[200] and the Supreme Court has accepted the phrase as a proper one.[201] While there has long been a lively debate as to what the separation of church and state means, and particularly over the question as to whether the scope of separation is limited to the implementation of religious freedom, there can be no disputing the fact that the concept of separation is securely anchored in prevailing federal and state court decisions.

It hardly needs argument to point out that the principle of separation is not designed to hinder or hurt religion. If separation means that the state may not support the churches through the direct grant of tax money, it is also true that separation means that the state may not lawfully interfere with the churches. If separation spares the state the heavy burden of sectarian controversy, it also frees the churches from the equally heavy burden of political and partisan controversy. Of course no one would even pretend that in our country the churches lack political influence,[202] but political power is another matter. As a Wisconsin Supreme Court judge once wrote, in a famous case dealing with Bible-reading, "There is no such source and cause of strife, quarrel, fights, malignant opposition, persecution, and war, and all evil in the state, as religion. Let it once enter into our civil affairs, our government would soon be destroyed."[203] He added that "religion needs no support from the state. It is stronger and much purer without it. . . . The connection of church and state corrupts religion, and makes the state despotic."[204]

Tax Exemptions. Perhaps religion needs no support from the state, but in actual fact the state in America has always extended many different kinds of support to religion, and indeed, in the early years of the republic direct public aid to religion, by way of support for churches and religious instruction, was common and generally accepted as legal.[205]

---

199 Wisc. Const. art. X, §§ 3, 6.
200 Letter to the Danbury Baptist Assoc., January 1, 1802, 16 Jefferson's Works 281 (Monticello ed. 1903). See Waite, Jefferson's "Wall of Separation": What and Where?, 33 Minn. L. Rev. 494 (1949).
201 See Everson v. Board of Educ., 330 U.S. 1, 16 (1947); Reynolds v. United States, 98 U.S. 145, 164 (1878).
202 See Billington, The Protestant Crusade, 1800-1860 (1938); Ebersole, Church Lobbying in the Nation's Capital (1951); Odegard, Religion and Politics (1960).
203 State ex rel. Weiss v. District Board, 76 Wis. 177, 219, 44 N.W. 967, 981 (1890) (concurring opinion).
204 Id. at 221, 44 N.W. at 981-82.
205 See the opinion of Chief Justice Jeremiah Smith in Muzzy v. Wilkins, 3 N.H. (Smith) 1 (1803); of Chief Justice Theophilus Parsons in Barnes v. Inhabitants of the First Parish, 6 Mass. (6 Tyng) 401 (1810); Inhabitants of Alna

Above all, throughout the course of American history down to the present day, American federal and state tax laws have extended the valuable privilege of exemption to religious societies.[206] Various types of exemptions favoring religious institutions are found in federal and state laws relating to taxes on property, income, inheritances, estates, gifts, sales, admissions, and the like. Thus the federal income tax statute permits the taxpayer to deduct, within certain limits, "any charitable contribution,"[207] and more specifically, to any organization "organized and operated exclusively for religious, charitable, scientific, literary, or educational purposes," provided that no part of its net earnings "inures to the benefit of any private shareholder or individual," and that "no substantial part" of its activities "is carrying on propaganda, or otherwise attempting, to influence legislation."[208] The fair rental value of a parsonage to a minister is also exempt from the federal income tax.[209] Similar exemptions for religious institutions are to be found in the federal statutes relating to estate taxes,[210] gift taxes,[211] admission taxes,[212] social security taxes,[213] and the unemployment compensation tax.[214] State tax laws on these subjects make similar exemptions for religious institutions, and in addition all states exempt church property, both real and personal, from general property taxes.[215]

American courts invariably sustain this tax exemption on public policy grounds. It is maintained that government should foster the teaching of religion because it improves the moral tone of the community.[216] It is also pointed out that the churches confer benefits upon the

---

v. Plummer, 3 Me. 88 (1824); O'Brien, Has Government an Interest in Religion?, 5 Vill. L. Rev. 335 (1960).

206 In addition, the Supreme Court has ruled that direct taxation of any religious activity, by way of the imposition of license fees, is a violation of the "free exercise" clause of the first amendment. Cantwell v. Connecticut, 310 U.S. 296 (1940); Murdock v. Pennsylvania, 319 U.S. 105 (1943).

207 Int. Rev. Code of 1954, § 170(a)(1).

208 Int. Rev. Code of 1954, § 170(c)(2)(B)(C)(D). For the regulations setting out the tests to qualify as an exempt organization see Treas. Reg. § 1.501(c)(3)-1 (1954).

209 Int. Rev. Code of 1954, § 107(1).

210 Int. Rev. Code of 1954, § 2055(a)(2)(3).

211 Int. Rev. Code of 1954, § 2522(a).

212 Int. Rev. Code of 1954, § 1701(a)(1)(A)(i).

213 Int. Rev. Code of 1954, § 1426(b)(8).

214 Int. Rev. Code of 1954, § 1607(c)(8).

215 See Stimson, The Exemption of Churches from Taxation, 18 Taxes 361-64, 397 (1940); Van Alstyne, Tax Exemption of Church Property, 20 Ohio St. L.J. 461 (1959); Symposium, Law and Philanthropy, 46 Va. L. Rev. 391 (1960); Note, 29 St. John's L. Rev. 121 (1954). Many other types of state statutes include exemptions for religious institutions, such as fair employment practices acts, labor relations acts, and workmen's compensation acts. Similar exemptions are found in the common law. For example, there is an old English common law rule that religious institutions are immune from ordinary rules of tort liability. The courts of about twenty states, however, have ruled that they are now subject to customary rules of negligence litigation. See Dalton v. St. Luke's Catholic Church, 27 N.J. 22, 141 A.2d 273 (1958).

216 Leading cases are: Garrett Biblical Institute v. Elmhurst State Bank, 331

public which to some extent relieve the burdens of the state in relation to the protection and advancement of the interests of its citizens.[217] Thus the Nebraska Supreme Court once declared: "As is said by many eminent authorities, the exemptions are granted on the hypothesis that the association or organization is of benefit to society, that it promotes the social and moral welfare, and, to some extent, is bearing burdens that would otherwise be imposed upon the public to be met by general taxation, and that from these considerations the exemption is granted."[218] It is also noted that if the policy of the state is to help all charitable institutions—as it is—then to omit religious institutions would be an unwarranted discrimination against religion and a restraint upon the free exercise of religion.[219] On the other hand, the exemption of church property from taxation has often been criticized,[220] and the argument is now being advanced that the recent Supreme Court decisions on the separation of church and state support the view that tax exemption is an unconstitutional aid to religion.[221] Thus a competent legal scholar has asserted that "there is no practical difference between making appropriations and failing to send a tax bill. In either event the church is given aid by the state."[222] Nevertheless, this writer recognized that against all the argument to the contrary "stands the force of American history."[223]

Undoubtedly the privilege of exemption from taxation is an aid to religion, and whether this aid is direct or indirect would not appear to have any serious economic significance. But the involvement of religion

---

Ill. 308, 163 N.E. 1 (1928); Trustees of Griswold College v. Iowa, 46 Iowa 275 (1877). See Kauper, The Constitutionality of Tax Exemption for Religious Activities, The Wall between Church and State, 95-116 (Oaks ed. 1963); Torpey, Judicial Doctrines of Religious Rights in America ch. 6 (1948). For recent decisions see: Lundberg v. County of Alameda, 46 Cal. 2d 644, 298 P.2d 1 (1956), appeal dismissed, 352 U.S. 921 (1956); General Fin. Corp. v. Archetto, 176 A.2d 73 (R.I. 1961), cert. denied, 369 U.S. 423 (1962).
[217] See Book Agents of Methodist Episcopal Church v. Hinton, 92 Tenn. 188, 21 S.W. 321 (1893); Trustees of First Methodist Church v. Atlanta, 76 Ga. 181 (1886).
[218] Y.M.C.A. v. Douglas Co., 60 Neb. 642, 646, 83 N.W. 924, 926 (1900). See Zabel, God and Caesar in Nebraska ch. 9 (1955).
[219] See Katz, Freedom of Religion and State Neutrality, 20 U. Chi. L. Rev. 426 (1953).
[220] See Mowry, Ought Church Property To Be Taxed?, 15 Green Bag 414 (1903).
[221] See Paulsen, Preferment of Religious Institutions in Tax and Labor Legislation, 14 Law & Contemp. Prob. 144 (1949); Pfeffer, Church, State, and Freedom 183 (1953); Note, 49 Colum. L. Rev. 968 (1949).
[222] Paulsen, supra note 221, at 147. Mr. Chief Justice Baldwin said, in Snyder v. Town of Newton, 147 Conn. 374, 386, 161 A.2d 770, 776 (1960), appeal dismissed, 365 U.S. 299 (1961): "Exemption from taxation is the equivalent of an appropriation of public funds, because the burden of the tax is lifted from the back of the potential taxpayer who is exempted and shifted to the backs of others." This remark was not intended to indicate disapproval of tax exemptions for churches, but merely as an objective description of what they are.
[223] Paulsen, supra note 221, at 147.

with the state goes much beyond this point, because once the state has adopted the policy of extending tax benefits to churches, it assumes the inescapable responsibility of deciding what a church is. Of course "the law does not profess to know what is a right belief,"[224] but it would be unthinkable if any group or institution could be allowed a tax exemption merely by claiming a religious label.[225] It follows that from the moment that the state decides to help the churches through exemption from taxes, it is involved with the churches because it must decide just what constitutes a bona fide church. Furthermore, as the Tax Court ruled in 1962, claimed deductions for gifts to religious organizations must be substantiated, and it observed that this rule was not an interference with religious freedom.[226]

That secular courts are inescapably involved in deciding what is a bona fide religious organization, when called upon to construe the coverage of statutory provisions for tax exemption, is attested to by judicial experience. Thus, the Court of Appeals for the Ninth Circuit recently ruled that a restaurant operated for profit does not become a church merely because it is called "Christ's Church of the Golden Rule" and the hired hands are called student ministers.[227] The court regarded this as a commercial enterprise even though the manager purported to "instruct" the student ministers in the faith, and even though the owner donated all of his gross receipts to the "church," which paid back the cost of operations plus subsistence. The court was not impressed with the argument that conducting commercial activities was a way of demonstrating and teaching the principles of religion.

Similarly, the Kentucky court recently refused to grant exemption from the property tax to a one-man organization known as the Mordecai F. Ham Evangelistic Association.[228] The property in question was the house in which Ham lived. Ham was independent of any religious denomination, being supported by voluntary contributors who responded to his evangelistic services over the radio. The court held that this was not a "religious society" within the meaning of the statute, but merely the alter ego of one man. The court said that a religious society is a church, a group organized and maintained for the support of public

---

224 In re Doyle, 16 Mo. App. 159, 166 (1884).
225 Tax exemption laws raise all sorts of issues of interpretation, as in the case of property tax exemptions. Courts must decide, for example, whether the statute includes the parsonage, State v. Church of Incarnation, 158 Minn. 48, 196 N.W. 802 (1924); a dormitory, State v. Carleton College, 154 Minn. 280, 191 N.W. 400 (1923); or an endowment fund invested in real estate mortgages, State v. Bishop Seabury Mission, 43 Minn. 344, 45 N.W. 615 (1890).
226 Lingenfelder v. Commissioner, 38 T.C. 44 (1962).
227 Riker v. Commissioner, 244 F.2d 220 (9th Cir.), cert. denied, 355 U.S. 839 (1957).
228 Mordecai F. Ham Evangelistic Ass'n v. Matthews, 300 Ky. 402, 189 S.W.2d 524 (1945).

worship. "If the property should be held exempt under these circumstances," the court declared, "the decision would afford a facility or means for any individual engaged in religious service to escape payment of taxes on his residence."[229] More recently the Kansas court denied exemption to the merchandise inventory, moneys and credits of the Baptist Book Store in Wichita, even though it served churches and Sunday schools and devoted its income to religious purposes.[230] The court ruled that this was a business activity, since the property was not used exclusively for religious purposes within the meaning of the state constitutional exemption. The Wisconsin court has ruled that the property of a hospital is not exempt from taxation merely because some religious services are conducted there, since it concluded that these activities were only incidental to the conduct of the corporate business.[231] The court held that under the statute a religious corporation must have a membership maintaining regular public worship in connection with a church. In 1960 the highest court of Montana denied the religious tax exemption to a communally-operated ranch on the ground that it was a purely commercial undertaking even though the members claimed to be a religious group animated by religious principles.[232] The Iowa court has denied exemption to a college fraternity house which was claimed on the theory that its articles of incorporation said that its purpose was "to promote the general moral, social, educational and literary welfare" of its members.[233] The issue, the court pointed out, is not determined by what the charter declares but by the use of the property, and its dominant use was that of a boarding house. The court was persuaded that the evidence showed that "any literary or scientific purposes . . . were merely incidental."[234] The Connecticut court has ruled that a retreat house for retired ministers was not within the statutory exemption of "houses of religious worship," even though it had a small chapel and was operated on a non-profit basis, and was the scene of daily prayers and the discussion of religious topics.[235] The Illinois court reached a similar conclusion in reference to a monastery which served as a

---

[229] Id. at 409-10, 189 S.W.2d at 528.

[230] Sunday School Bd. of Southern Baptist Convention v. McCue, 179 Kan. 1, 293 P.2d 234 (1956).

[231] United States Nat'l Bank v. Poor Handmaids of Jesus Christ, 148 Wisc. 613, 135 N.W. 121 (1912).

[232] State v. King Colony Ranch, 137 Mont. 145, 350 P.2d 841, cert. denied, 364 U.S. 817 (1960).

[233] Theta Xi Bldg. Ass'n v. Board of Review, 217 Iowa 1181, 251 N.W. 76 (1933).

[234] Id. at 1185, 251 N.W. at 78. College fraternities have fared badly in their quest for tax exemption. See People v. Alpha Pi, 326 Ill. 573, 158 N.E. 213 (1927); Knox College v. Board of Review, 308 Ill. 160, 139 N.E. 56 (1923); Orono v. Sigma Alpha Epsilon Soc'y, 105 Me. 214, 74 Atl. 19 (1909); Phi Beta Epsilon v. City of Boston, 182 Mass. 457, 65 N.E. 824 (1903).

[235] Town of Woodstock v. The Retreat, Inc., 125 Conn. 52, 3 A.2d 232 (1938).

home for a contemplative order of nuns (St. Clare) who have re-
nounced all connection with the public, never leave the cloisters, and
do not talk except in limited recreation periods.[236] The court ruled that
tax exemption is not a mere gift to religion, but rather that the reason
for it was some general public benefit, such as public worship or religious instruction.

The Connecticut court has ruled that a Masonic Temple is not a
"house of religious worship,[237] and the Nebraska court once ruled that
way also,[238] but a decade later it changed its mind, holding that the
Masonic Order had both educational and religious purposes, and that
contrary to the view of the trial court, the profession of a sectarian
creed is not an essential element of a "religious use."[239] But in exempt-
ing the Masonic Temple the court stressed the charitable uses of the
organization, though it found that there were also religious uses within
the meaning of the statute. Courts have ruled in favor of tax exemption
in behalf of a variety of organizations, including the Y.M.C.A.,[240] an
"I Am" reading room,[241] and the Methodist Board of Temperance,
Prohibition and Public Morals, which, it was stressed, was subject to
the control of the General Conference.[242] In 1962, a federal district court
allowed deductions for contributions to a church which for doctrinal
reasons had no distinctive name or written by-laws, no permanent
headquarters or comprehensive records, but the members of which held
regular public meetings in homes and rented quarters, under the
guidance of ministers and church officers.[243] In 1926 the Board of Tax
Appeals, (now called the Tax Court) extended income tax exemptions
to a Unity School of Christianity which believed in faith healing, silent
prayer, vegetarianism and spiritualism.[244] The Board declared that "religion is not confined to a sect or a ritual. The symbols of religion to
one are anathema to another. What one may regard as charity another
may scorn as foolish waste." On the other hand, another federal district
court once denied the claim of a taxpayer who had made a gift to the
"Freethinkers of America, Inc.," on the ground that its main function
was to conduct litigation to prevent the expenditure of public money for

---

[236] People v. Muldoon, 306 Ill. 234, 137 N.E. 863 (1922).
[237] Masonic Bldg. Ass'n v. Town of Stamford, 119 Conn. 53, 174 Atl. 301 (1934).
[238] Scottish Rite Bldg. Co. v. Lancaster County, 106 Neb. 95, 182 N.W. 574
(1921). The court held that there was a clear distinction between ethical teachings
and the doctrines of religion.
[239] Ancient & Accepted Scottish Rite v. Board of County Comm'rs, 122 Neb.
586, 241 N.W. 93 (1932).
[240] Commonwealth v. Y.M.C.A., 116 Ky. 711, 76 S.W. 522 (1903). The court
held that the lack of an ordained minister and departure from customary modes of
worship were not decisive facts in reaching a determination.
[241] Potter v. United States, 79 F. Supp. 297 (N.D. Ill. 1946).
[242] Girard Trust Co. v. Commissioner, 122 F.2d 108 (3d Cir. 1941).
[243] Morey v. Riddell, 205 F. Supp. 918 (S.D. Cal. 1962).
[244] Unity School of Christianity, 4 B.T.A. 61 (1926).

the promotion of religion.[245] Such an organization, the court ruled, was not engaged exclusively in the pursuit of charitable, educational or scientific objectives within the meaning of the federal estate tax law.

Perhaps the most interesting of the tax exemption issues is the question as to whether a belief in God, or at least in some sort of divinity, is a legally necessary element of the definition of a church. On this question a variety of views has been expressed. Of the nine definitions given in the second edition of Webster's unabridged *New International Dictionary* (1955), eight are in terms of faith in a supreme being.[246] Justice Field asserted that religion "has reference to one's views of his relations to his Creator,"[247] and Chief Justice Hughes once said that "the essence of religion is belief in a relation to God involving duties superior to those arising from any human relation."[248] The Chief Judge of the Federal District Court for the Southern District of California, Leon R. Yankwich, has taken the position that while there is dispute among students as to what religion is, what Congress had in mind in using the term in the Selective Service Act was "the relationship of the individual to a Supreme Being."[249]

There were two cases decided in 1957, one in the court of appeals of the District of Columbia,[250] and one in a California district court of appeals,[251] which posed the issue as to whether a belief in God, or some supreme being, was required to qualify for the religious tax exemp-

---

[245] Old Colony Trust Co. v. Welch, 25 F. Supp. 45 (D. Mass. 1938).

[246] The fifth definition is: "Devotion or fidelity; scrupulous conformity; conscientiousness." More typical is the first: "The service or adoration of God or a god as expressed in forms of worship, in obedience to divine commands, especially as found in accepted sacred writings or as declared by recognized teachers and in the pursuit of a way of life regarded as incumbent on true believers . . . ." Webster, New International Dictionary 2105 (unab. ed. 1962).

[247] Davis v. Beason, 133 U.S. 333, 342 (1890).

[248] United States v. Macintosh, 283 U.S. 605, 633 (1931) (dissenting opinion). See People v. Board of Educ., 245 Ill. 334, 340, 92 N.E. 251, 252 (1910); "Religion has reference to man's relation to divinity; to the moral obligation of reverence and worship, obedience and submission."

[249] George v. United States, 196 F.2d 445, 451 (9th Cir.), cert. denied, 344 U.S. 843 (1952). For similar definitions see: People v. Deutsche Evangelische Lutherische Jehovah Geneinde, 249 Ill. 132, 136, 94 N.E. 162, 164 (1911): "it means the formal recognition of God . . ."; Nikulnikoff v. Archbishop of Russian Orthodox Church, 142 Misc. 894, 255 N.Y.S. 653, 663 (Sup. Ct. 1932): "Religion as generally accepted may be defined as a bond uniting man to God . . ."; Cline v. State, 9 Okla. Crim. 40, 130 Pac. 510 (1913); Berman v. United States, 156 F.2d 377 (9th Cir.), cert. denied, 329 U.S. 795 (1946); Opinion of the Justices, 309 Mass. 555, 34 N.E.2d 431 (1941). William James defined religion as "the feelings, acts, and experiences of individual men in their solitude, so far as they apprehend themselves to stand in relation to whatever they may consider the divine." James, The Varieties of Religious Experience 31 (1923). Professor Alfred Bertholet of the University of Berlin defined religion as "the complex of man's interrelations with the superhuman powers." 13 Encyclopedia of the Social Sciences 229 (1934).

[250] Washington Ethical Soc'y v. District of Columbia, 249 F.2d 127 (D.C. Cir. 1957).

[251] Fellowship of Humanity v. County of Alameda, 153 Cal. App. 2d 673, 315 P.2d 394 (1957).

tions.[252] In the former case the tax assessor and the tax court of the district had decided that the Washington Ethical Society, which does not believe in God, was not within the meaning of an act of Congress which exempted from property taxation "religious corporations or societies." By unanimous vote the United States Court of Appeals for the District of Columbia reversed, noting that the Society held regular Sunday services which followed customary forms of service, and had "leaders" who preached and ministered to members in such matters as marriage and burial. The Court declared that the term "religion" is not a fixed concept, and that in granting tax exemption, Congress, like most state legislatures, "was giving expression to a broad legislative purpose to grant support to elements in the community regarded as good for the community."[253] In fact, the Court said that "to construe exemptions so strictly that unorthodox or minority forms of worship would be denied the exemption benefits granted to those conforming to the majority beliefs might well raise constitutional issues."[254]

The California case involved the Fellowship of Humanity in Oakland. Here the court pointed out that there are forms of belief generally accepted as religious, and having millions of adherents, which do not require a belief in a deity as essential. Taoism, classic Buddhism and Confucianism were cited as illustrations. The court found that the dictionary definitions of religion were not conclusive, and declared that it would not be consistent with our tradition of religious tolerance to follow a narrow definition. The court ruled that it would not be proper for civil authorities to examine the validity of religious beliefs. This being so, it held that only an objective test would suffice. It concluded that objectively a religion must include the following: a belief, though not necessarily involving supernatural powers; a cult; a system of moral practice based on the belief; and an organization designed for the observance of the tenets of the belief. With this sort of test, the court concluded, whether the beliefs of the Fellowship of Humanity are theistic or not becomes clearly immaterial.

Whether these courts were right or wrong in holding non-theistic societies to be entitled to tax exemption is not the issue posed in this discussion, though it is an interesting question to debate. The point is that even when the state shows its friendliest face to religion by giving churches the very valuable privilege of exemption from general taxation, it gets involved with religion because it must make an independent inquiry as to the merits of any particular claim to tax exemption. Thus

---

[252] See Note, 58 Colum. L. Rev. 417 (1958) ; Comment, 7 De Paul L. Rev. 206 (1958).
[253] Washington Ethical Soc'y v. District of Columbia, 249 F.2d 127, 129 (D.C. Cir. 1957).
[254] Ibid.

the lay judges of the civil power, in spite of our commitment to the separation of church and state, must decide what constitutes a religion, and what is a church. The alternative would be an open invitation to charlatans, tax-dodgers and fiscal chaos.

Military Service. American courts get involved in similar problems when they are called upon to construe federal legislation which grants exemption from the obligation to perform military service on religious grounds. The Draft Act of 1917[255] exempted duly ordained ministers and theological students, and excused from combatant service those conscientious objectors who were members of "any well-recognized religious sect or organization at present organized and existing and whose existing creed or principles forbid its members to participate in war in any form. . . ." This had reference to the so-called historic peace churches, such as the Friends, Mennonite and Brethren churches. The Supreme Court made short shrift of the argument that an establishment of religion resulted from the exemption clauses of the Act, declaring that the argument was so apparently unsound that it was only necessary to state it.[256] The Selective Service Act of 1940 expanded the religious exemption by extending it to any conscientious objector "who, by reason of religious training and belief, is conscientiously opposed to participation in war in any form. . . ."[257] Then the Universal Military Training and Service Act of 1948 added: "Religious training and belief in this connection means an individual's belief in a relation to a Supreme Being involving duties superior to those arising from any human relation, but does not include essentially political, sociological, or philosophical views or a merely personal moral code."[258] The present statute also exempts "regular or duly ordained ministers of religion, . . . and students preparing for the ministry under the direction of recognized churches or religious organizations. . . ."[259]

When in 1948 Congress undertook to define what "religious training and belief" means, it was argued that this constituted an establishment of religion, but this contention was brushed aside on the authority of the Supreme Court decision which sustained the 1917 statute.[260] It was pointed out that the right to be exempt from military service does not come from the Constitution, but rather from Congress, and thus Con-

---

[255] 40 Stat. 76 (1917).
[256] Selective Draft Law Cases (Arver v. United States), 245 U.S. 366, 390 (1918). See also: United States v. Herling, 120 F.2d 236 (2d Cir. 1941).
[257] 54 Stat. 885 (1940).
[258] Universal Military Training & Service Act, 62 Stat. 609 (1948), 50 App. U.S.C. § 456(j) (1958).
[259] Universal Military Training & Service Act, 62 Stat. 609 (1948), 50 App. U.S.C. § 456(g) (1958).
[260] George v. United States, 196 F.2d 445 (9th Cir.), cert. denied, 344 U.S. 843 (1952).

52

gress is free to deny exemption to any persons whose opinions Congress does not choose to classify as "religious." Furthermore, it was held that the 1948 amendment, which "is couched in terms of the relationship of the individual to a Supreme Being," was consistent with the spirit in which "religion" is generally understood.[261]

This legislation, which, like tax exemption legislation, emanates from a spirit which is friendly to religion, necessarily involves administrative officers of the state and reviewing courts in making many decisions regarding the sincerity or genuineness of claims for exemption.[262] This is inescapable, since the alternative—to grant a claim on religious grounds merely for the asking—is wholly unthinkable. Thus, a mere claim that one is a minister of religion is not final, and is subject to judicial review.[263] Courts have refused, for example, to accept the claim of Jehovah's Witnesses that every member of the sect is a minister of religion within the meaning of the statute.[264] Furthermore, it is well settled that Congress has the constitutional power to require some sort of non-combatant service from those who are given exemption from military service because of religious conviction.[265] "The rights of religion are not beyond limitation," a federal court of appeals has declared. "The guaranty of freedom of religion in the Bill of Rights is not a guaranty of immunity for violation of law."[266] For, as another court of appeals has pointed out, to permit religious belief to serve as a justification for violation of the law "would be to make the professed doctrine

---

[261] Id. at 451.

[262] See Freeman, A Remonstrance for Conscience, 106 U. Penn. L. Rev. 806 (1958) ; Heisler, The Law Versus the Conscientious Objector, 20 U. Chi. L. Rev. 441 (1953) ; Irion, The Legal Status of the Conscientious Objector, 8 Geo. Wash. L. Rev. 125 (1939) ; Jacob, Religious Freedom—A Good Security Risk?, 300 Annals 41 (1955) ; McCown, Conscience v. The State, 32 Calif. L. Rev. 1 (1944).

[263] See Dickinson v. United States, 346 U.S. 389 (1953) ; United States v. Mohammed, 288 F.2d 236 (7th Cir. 1961) ; Wiggins v. United States, 261 F.2d 113 (5th Cir. 1958), cert. denied, 359 U.S. 942 (1959) ; Bradshaw v. United States, 242 F.2d 180 (10th Cir. 1957) ; Leitner v. United States, 222 F.2d 363 (4th Cir. 1955) ; Martin v. United States, 190 F.2d 775 (4th Cir. 1951), cert. denied, 342 U.S. 872 (1951).

[264] See Gonzales v. United States, 364 U.S. 59 (1960) ; Dickinson v. United States, supra note 263; Cox v. United States, 332 U.S. 442 (1947) ; United States v. Hoepker, 223 F.2d 921 (7th Cir. 1955), cert. denied, 350 U.S. 841 (1955) ; United States v. Mroz, 136 F.2d 221 (7th Cir. 1943) ; Rase v. United States, 129 F.2d 204 (6th Cir. 1942) ; Sibley & Jacob, Conscription of Conscience (1952) ; Tietz, Jehovah's Witnesses: Conscientious Objectors, 20 So. Cal. L. Rev. 123 (1955).

[265] Reese v. United States, 225 F.2d 766 (9th Cir. 1955) ; Roodenko v. United States, 147 F.2d 752 (10th Cir. 1944), cert. denied, 324 U.S. 860 (1945) ; United States v. Bartell, 144 F. Supp. 793 (S.D.N.Y. 1956) ; United States v. Lebherz, 129 F. Supp. 444 (D. N.J. 1955).

[266] Gara v. United States, 178 F.2d 38, 40 (1949), aff'd by an evenly divided court, 340 U.S. 857 (1950). Here the court upheld a conviction of one who had counselled another to refuse to register for the draft on religious grounds. To the same effect are Warren v. United States, 177 F.2d 596 (10th Cir. 1949) ; Baxley v. United States, 134 F.2d 937 (4th Cir. 1943).

of religious belief superior to the law of the land and in effect would permit every objector to become a law unto himself."[267]

While one who claims for himself the status of a conscientious objector has a right to be heard on that issue before an administrative body, though the hearing can be something less than the full hearing which must be available in the normal course of litigation,[268] nevertheless the administrative authorities and reviewing courts may inquire into the nature and sincerity of the asserted religious beliefs.[269] The Supreme Court has pointed out that the ultimate issue in conscientious objector cases is the sincerity and good faith belief of the registrant, and thus, where the registrant claimed three different classifications at various times, an inference of insincerity was warranted, since "even firemen become dubious after two false alarms."[270] Courts have upheld administrative decisions denying the exemption where the registrant rests his claim to being classified as a conscientious objector on the basis of a personal humanistic or political philosophy, since he is not the kind of objector whom the statute was designed to exclude.[271] In making decisions of this sort, judges get involved in the effort to determine just what religion means. Thus Judge Stephens, of the Ninth Circuit, has written that the statute was written "for the specific purpose of distinguishing between a conscientious social belief, or a sincere devotion to a high moralistic philosophy, and one based upon an individual's belief in his responsibility to an authority higher and beyond any worldly one."[272] He thought it would be "quite ridiculous" to argue that the authors of the first amendment could have used the word "religion" as "meaning to be inclusive of morals or of devotion to human welfare or of policy of government. Congress has and does make laws respecting the establishment of all of these subjects."[273] He did not mean to say that man's comprehension of religion is static. Nevertheless, "all discoveries of science and the deepest reach of minds do not fill a life or satisfy the soul hunger to understand the daily joys and sadnesses and disappointments of life or to understand the ultimate pur-

---

[267] United States v. Kime, 188 F.2d 677 (7th Cir. 1951), cert. denied, 342 U.S. 823 (1951).

[268] United States v. Nugent, 346 U.S. 1 (1953).

[269] Sicurella v. United States, 348 U.S. 385 (1955); United States v. Erikson, 149 F. Supp. 576 (S.D.N.Y. 1957).

[270] Witmer v. United States, 348 U.S. 375, 383 (1955).

[271] Clark v. United States, 236 F.2d 13 (9th Cir.), cert. denied, 352 U.S. 882 (1956); Davidson v. United States, 225 F.2d 836 (9th Cir.), cert. denied, 350 U.S. 887 (1955); Imboden v. United States, 194 F.2d 508 (6th Cir.), cert. denied, 343 U.S. 957 (1952); Berman v. United States, 156 F.2d 377 (9th Cir.), cert. denied, 329 U.S. 795 (1946); United States v. Kauten, 133 F.2d 703 (2d Cir. 1943). But cf. United States v. Badt, 141 F.2d 845 (2d Cir. 1944), where Judge Hand ruled that religious belief did not necessarily connote some concept of deity.

[272] Berman v. United States, supra note 271, at 380.

[273] Ibid.

pose of creation. Faith in a supreme power above and beyond the law of all creation mollifies our fears and satisfies our longings."[274] Judge Stephens concluded that no matter how pure and admirable one's philosophy may be, "without the concept of deity [it] cannot be said to be religion" in the sense in which the term is used in the statute.[275]

A registrant may be entitled to the conscientious objector classification even if he is not a member of any particular religious sect or organization,[276] and it is error to deny the exemption to a registrant merely because he belongs to a church which does not preach pacifism.[277] On the other hand, if he ascribes his beliefs to the church of which he is a member, then administrative officials and courts will inquire into the tenets of this church to determine for themselves whether it does in fact hold the views ascribed to it.[278]

There are other situations which involve the courts in the making of judgments about religion in reference to some aspect of military service. Thus courts have upheld compulsory R.O.T.C. training in colleges and universities over religious objections.[279] The New York Court of Appeals recently held that one may, over religious objections, constitutionally be compelled to take shelter during an air raid drill conducted pursuant to the State Defense Emergency Act.[280] The Supreme Court has ruled, though by a 5-4 vote, that a state may refuse to admit a conscientious objector to the bar, even though the applicant

---

[274] Ibid. Cf. the remarks of Judge Hand in United States v. Kauten, 133 F.2d 703, 708 (2d Cir. 1943) : "Religious belief arises from a sense of the inadequacy of reason as a means of relating the individual to his fellow-men and to his universe— a sense common to men in the most primitive and in the most highly civilized societies. It accepts the aid of logic but refuses to be limited by it. It is a belief finding expression in a conscience which categorically requires the believer to disregard elementary self-interest and to accept martyrdom in preference to transgressing its tenets."

[275] 156 F.2d at 380. Judge Denman argued in dissent that "many of the great religious faiths with hundreds of millions of followers have no god," citing as examples Taoism, Buddhism and Comte's religion of humanism. Id. at 384.

[276] United States v. Alvies, 112 F. Supp. 618 (N.D. Cal. 1953).

[277] United States v. Everngam, 102 F. Supp. 128 (S.D. W. Va. 1951).

[278] Roberson v. United States, 208 F.2d 166 (10th Cir. 1953) ; Head v. United States, 199 F.2d 337 (10th Cir. 1952), cert. denied, 345 U.S. 910 (1953). Both of these cases dealt with members of the Church of Christ.

[279] The leading case is Hamilton v. Regents of Univ. of Cal., 293 U.S. 245 (1934). Said Justice Cardozo, in a concurring opinion, at 268: "The conscientious objector, if his liberties were to be thus extended, might refuse to contribute taxes in furtherance of war, whether for attack or for defense, or in furtherance of any other end condemned by his conscience as irreligious or immoral. The right of private judgment has never yet been so exalted above the powers and the compulsion of the agencies of government. One who is a martyr to a principle—which may turn out in the end to be a delusion or an error—does not prove by his martyrdom that he has kept within the law." For other cases upholding compulsory R.O.T.C. programs see, Hanauer v. Elkins, 217 Md. 213, 141 A.2d 903 (1958) ; Pearson v. Coale, 165 Md. 224, 167 Atl. 54, appeal dismissed, 290 U.S. 597 (1933).

[280] People v. Peck, 195 N.Y.S.2d 637, 163 N.E.2d 866 (1959). See also, People v. Parilli, 1 Misc. 2d 201, 499, 147 N.Y.S.2d 618 (Mag. Ct. 1955).

grounded his position upon religious convictions.[281] The Supreme Court once took the position that a religious or other pacifist could not qualify for citizenship under the Naturalization Act,[282] but later held that even a pacifist could "support and defend" the Constitution, as the statute required, since one may defend his country by other than military means.[283] Congress removed the statutory ambiguity when it enacted the Naturalization Act of 1952,[284] for now a pacifist may take the oath of allegiance and become a citizen provided that he can show "by clear and convincing evidence to the satisfaction of the naturalization court that he is opposed to the bearing of arms in the Armed Forces of the United States by reason of religious training and belief." The statute goes on to specify that "the term 'religious training and belief' as used in this section shall mean an individual's belief in a relation to a Supreme Being involving duties superior to those arising from any human relation, but does not include essentially political, sociological, or philosophical views or a merely personal moral code." Of course, the judges must decide whether a pacifist applicant for naturalization qualifies under the statute. Thus it has been held that a member of the Mennonite Brethren Church is entitled to take the pacifist's oath on naturalization,[285] but that a member of the Lutheran Church and German Christian Endeavor Society could not qualify since neither taught pacifism.[286] One may qualify as having the requisite "religious training and belief," however, even though he is not a member of a church committed to pacifism.[287]

Family Relationships. A considerable number of family relationships which are subject in some significant way to the control of law also involve religious considerations which the law must take into account. Thus, in this important area of conduct the secular judges of the state, despite the principle of the separation of church and state, get involved in the making of judgments about various aspects of religion. These issues arise in connection with such matters as the award of child custody, adoption, antenuptial agreements regarding the religious training of offspring, divorce, and parental control over the religious education of children.[288]

---

[281] In re Summers, 325 U.S. 561 (1945).
[282] United States v. Macintosh, 283 U.S. 605 (1931); United States v. Schwimmer, 279 U.S. 644 (1929).
[283] Girouard v. United States, 328 U.S. 61 (1946). See also, Cohnstaedt v. Immigration & Naturalization Serv., 339 U.S. 901 (1950).
[284] 66 Stat. 258(a) (1952), 8 U.S.C. § 1448(a) (1958).
[285] Petition of Thiesen, 141 Cal. App. 2d 274, 296 P.2d 566 (1956).
[286] In re Nissen, 138 F. Supp. 483 (D. Mass. 1955), supplemental opinion, 138 F. Supp. 485 (D. Mass. 1956), noted in 56 Colum. L. Rev. 1233 (1956).
[287] In re Hansen, 148 F. Supp. 187 (D. Minn. 1957).
[288] See Paulsen, Constitutional Problems of Utilizing a Religious Factor in Adoptions and Placements of Children, in The Wall between Church and State

In awarding custody of children to a parent, following a separation, American courts usually hold that if the parent is otherwise qualified, the religious views of the parent do not matter.[289] Courts avoid getting involved in the task of weighing the relative merits of different religions.[290] Thus it has been repeatedly held that the fact that the parent is a Jehovah Witness does not warrant denial of child custody,[291] although there have been cases where religious beliefs have been taken into account where a serious detriment to the health of the child was involved.[292] In a recent case, for example, a New York court awarded custody of the child to the father because the religious beliefs of the mother on such medical matters as blood transfusions imposed a serious hazard upon the child.[293] There are also situations where the issue of custody is resolved in terms of an arrangement which would best insure the continued religious education and training of the child along established lines.[294]

Religion is also a factor, and often a decisive factor, in adoption cases. In 1955, in a widely-discussed case, the highest court of Massachusetts upheld a state statute[295] which bars adoption by couples of a different faith than that of the child's mother, by providing that the judge must follow the religious faith of the child "when practicable."[296] In this in-

---

117-41 (Oaks ed. 1963); Overton, Religion and Adoption, 23 Tenn. L. Rev. 951 (1955); Pfeffer, Religion in the Upbringing of Children, 35 B.U.L. Rev. 333 (1955); Note, 54 Colum. L. Rev. 376 (1954); Note, 64 Yale L.J. 772 (1956).

[289] Cory v. Cory, 70 Cal. App. 2d 563, 161 P.2d 385 (3d Dist. 1945); Jackson v. Jackson, 181 Kan. 1, 309 P.2d 705 (1957); Denton v. James, 107 Kan. 729, 193 Pac. 307 (1920); People ex rel. Portnoy v. Strasser, 303 N.Y. 539, 104 N.E.2d 895 (1952); People ex rel. Woolston v. Woolston, 135 Misc. 320, 239 N.Y.S. 185 (Sup. Ct. 1929).

[290] McLaughlin v. McLaughlin, 20 Conn. Supp. 274, 132 A.2d 420 (1957).

[291] Stone v. Stone, 90 Ariz. 190, 367 P.2d 230 (1961), noted in 4 Ariz. L. Rev. 298 (1963); Jackson v. Jackson, 181 Kan. 1, 304 P.2d 705 (1957), noted in 31 So. Cal. L. Rev. 313 (1958); Reynolds v. Rayborn, 116 S.W.2d 836 (Tex. Civ. App. 1938); Bond v. Bond, 144 W. Va. 478, 109 S.E.2d 16 (1959).

[292] Hardman v. Hardman, 308 Ky. 284, 214 S.W.2d 391 (1948); Gluckstern v. Gluckstern, 17 Misc. 2d 83, 158 N.Y.S.2d 504 (Sup. Ct. 1956), aff'd, 3 App. Div. 2d 432, 165 N.Y.S.2d 432 (1956), 4 N.Y.2d 521, 151 N.E.2d 897, 176 N.Y.S.2d 352 (1956); Commonwealth ex rel. Kaufman v. Kaufman, 69 Montg. Co. L.B. 292 (Pa. 1953).

[293] Battaglia v. Battaglia, 9 Misc. 2d 1067, 172 N.Y.S.2d 361 (Sup. Ct. 1958). In Salvaggio v. Barnett, 248 S.W.2d 244 (Tex. Civ. App. 1952), a decision to change custody from the father to the mother turned largely on the fact that the father assumed a body of religious beliefs which included teaching the child that it was wrong to salute the flag or celebrate Christmas.

[294] Dansker v. Dansker, 279 S.W.2d 205 (Mo. App. 1955); Ex parte De Bois, 7 N.J. Misc. 1029, 148 Atl. 10 (1929); Com. ex rel. Sabath v. Mendelson, 187 Pa. Sup. 73, 143 A.2d 665 (1958).

[295] Mass. Gen. Laws Ann. ch. 210, § 5B (1955).

[296] Petition of Goldman, 331 Mass. 647, 121 N.E.2d 843 (1954), cert. denied, 348 U.S. 942 (1955), noted in 53 Mich. L. Rev. 984 (1955), 7 Stan. L. Rev. 394 (1955). See also Ellis v. McCoy, 332 Mass. 254, 124 N.E.2d 266 (1955); Purinton v. Jamrock, 195 Mass. 187, 80 N.E. 802 (1907); Burrett & Broeder, The Impact of Religious Factors in Nebraska Adoptions, 38 Neb. L. Rev. 641 (1959); Ramsey, The Legal Imputation of Religion to an Infant in Adoption Proceedings, 34 N.Y.U.L. Rev. 649 (1959); Comment, 28 Ind. L.J. 401 (1953).

stance the court declined to permit the attempted adoption of the twin children of a Catholic by Jewish parents, who were otherwise well qualified in every way, even though the mother was not a practicing Catholic at the time and had consented to the arrangement. On the constitutional issue Chief Justice Qua declared: "All religions are treated alike. There is no 'subordination' of one sect to another. No burden is placed upon anyone for maintenance of any religion. No exercise of religion is required, prevented, or hampered."[297]

Chief Justice Qua also pointed out that the principle involved in this statute had received widespread approval. The New York statute, for example, provides, as does the Massachusetts law, that in adoption cases the religion of the child must be followed "when practicable,"[298] and the Illinois statute states "whenever possible."[299] The Illinois Supreme Court has ruled that while the court has discretion under the statute, it meant that religion should be given greater weight than the other factors.[300] The New York Court of Appeals took a similar position in 1958,[301] but the legislature promptly amended the statute to read that the religious requirement "shall be interpreted literally."[302] The Massachusetts statute has also been construed to vest discretionary authority in the judge.[303] In addition, some courts have taken the position that the main concern of the state is the welfare of the child, and that other considerations may well outweigh the religious factor in making a determination.[304] Finally, it should be noted that courts will often take religious factors into consideration when choosing guardians other than the natural parents,[305] though in many instances courts hold that religious considerations are not necessarily decisive.[306]

[297] Household Fuel Corp. v. Hamacher, 331 Mass. 652, 121 N.E.2d 846 (1954).
[298] N.Y. Family Court Act, § 116.
[299] Ill. Rev. Stat. ch. 4, § 9.1-15 (1961).
[300] Cooper v. Hinrichs, 10 Ill. 2d 269, 140 N.E.2d 293 (1957).
[301] Matter of Maxwell, 4 N.Y.2d 429, 151 N.E.2d 848 (1958), noted in 25 Brooklyn L. Rev. 334 (1959), 10 Syracuse L. Rev. 124 (1958), 6 U.C.L.A.L. Rev. 459 (1959); see also Adoption of Anonymous, 207 Misc. 240, 137 N.Y.S.2d 720 (1955); Matter of Santos, 278 App. Div. 373, 105 N.Y.S.2d 716 (1951); In re Korte, 78 Misc. 276, 139 N.Y.S. 444 (1912).
[302] N.Y. Family Court Act, § 116(d). See Note, 28 St. John's L. Rev. 276 (1954).
[303] Petition of Gally, 329 Mass. 143, 107 N.E.2d 21 (1952).
[304] Eggleston v. Landrum, 210 Miss. 645, 50 So. 2d 364 (1951); In re McKenzie, 197 Minn. 234, 266 N.W. 746 (1936).
[305] People ex rel. Flannery v. Bolton, 27 Colo. App. 39, 146 Pac. 489 (1915); State v. Young, 121 Neb. 619, 237 N.W. 677 (1931); In re McConnon, 60 Misc. 22, 112 N.Y.S. 560 (1908); Ex parte Agnello, 72 N.Y.S.2d 186 (Sup. Ct. 1947); In re Lamb's Estate, 139 N.Y.S. 685 (Surr. Ct. 1912). Cf. Sullivan v. Sullivan, 141 Conn. 235, 104 A.2d 898 (1954). See also, 66 A.L.R.2d 1410 (1959); 22 A.L.R.2d 696 (1953).
[306] In the Matter of Chandler, 170 Cal. App. 2d 606, 339 P.2d 183 (1959); In re Walker, 159 Cal. App. 2d 403, 324 P.2d 32 (1958); In re Walsh's Estate, 100 Cal. App. 2d 194, 223 P.2d 322 (1950); In re Duren, 355 Mo. 1222, 200 S.W.2d 343 (1943); In re Dixon, 254 Mo. 663, 163 S.W. 827 (1914); State ex rel. Baker v.

58

The Supreme Court has ruled that parents have a constitutionally protected right to educate their children in church-controlled schools if they so desire.[307] But at a certain point in life children are legally free to decide for themselves what religion they wish to practice. Thus New York courts have recently ruled that a boy of 12 or 13 may choose his own faith.[308] Until the age of choice is reached, however, it is well established that the parent or parents who have custody have the right to choose the religious training of the child,[309] and courts are reluctant or unwilling to take jurisdiction where the parents disagree over the religious education of their child, since "no end of difficulties would arise should judges try to tell parents how to bring up their children."[310] Similarly, where husband and wife enter into an antenuptial contract regarding the religious education of any children which may issue from the marriage, such an agreement is not judicially enforceable for the reason that a court decree would interfere with the parent's right of conscience.[311]

Finally, religion may be a factor in divorce proceedings.[312] Thus, a New Jersey court recently gave a wife a divorce because her husband made her life miserable to force his newly-found religion upon her.[313] It has also been held that conduct of one spouse to the other may be characterized as cruel even though actuated by religious beliefs.[314] A Texas court recently held that the fact that the wife

Bird, 253 Mo. 569, 162 S.W. 119 (1913); Commonwealth ex rel. Stevens v. Shannon, 107 Pa. Super. 557, 164 Atl. 352 (1933); cf. Scanlon v. Scanlon, 29 N.J. Sup. 317, 102 A.2d 656 (1954).

[307] Pierce v. Society of Sisters, 268 U.S. 510 (1925); Meyer v. Nebraska, 262 U.S. 390 (1923).

[308] Hehman v. Hehman, 13 Misc. 2d 318, 178 N.Y.S.2d 328 (Sup. Ct. 1958), noted in 59 Colum. L. Rev. 680 (1959); Martin v. Martin, 308 N.Y. 136, 123 N.E.2d 812 (1954), noted in 1 N.Y.L.F. 247 (1955); cf. Prieto v. St. Alphonsus Convent, 52 La. Ann. 631, 27 So. 153 (1900).

[309] Lindsay v. Lindsay, 257 Ill. 328, 100 N.E. 892 (1913); Lynch v. Uhlenhopp, 248 Iowa 68, 78 N.W.2d 491 (1956), noted in 42 Iowa L. Rev. 617 (1957), 34 N.C.L. Rev. 509 (1956); Wojnarowicz v. Wojnarowicz, 48 N.J. Super. 349, 137 A.2d 618 (1958); Donahue v. Donahue, 142 N.J. Eq. 701, 61 A.2d 243 (1948); Ex parte Kananack, 272 App. Div. 783, 69 N.Y.S.2d 886 (1947); Angel v. Angel, 140 N.E.2d 86 (Ohio Ct. Com. Pl. 1956); see Note, 3 De Paul L. Rev. 83 (1953).

[310] People ex rel. Sisson v. Sisson, 271 N.Y. 285, 287, 2 N.E.2d 660, 661 (1936).

[311] See McLaughlin v. McLaughlin, 20 Conn. Sup. 274, 132 A.2d 420 (1957); Stanton v. Stanton, 213 Ga. 545, 100 S.E.2d 289 (1957), noted in 46 Ky. L.J. 627 (1958); Boerger v. Boerger, 26 N.J. Super. 90, 97 A.2d 419 (1953); Martin v. Martin, 308 N.Y. 136, 123 N.E.2d 812 (1954); Hackett v. Hackett, 78 Ohio L. Abs. 485, 150 N.E.2d 431 (Ohio 1958), noted in 72 Harv. L. Rev. 372 (1958), 19 Ohio St. L.J. 483 (1958), 28 U. of Cinc. L. Rev. 375 (1959); Friedman, The Parental Right to Control the Religious Education of a Child, 29 Harv. L. Rev. 485 (1916); Martin, Enforceability of Ante-nuptial Promises to Raise Children in a Particular Religion, 3 N.H.B.J. 18 (1960); Note, 10 West. Res. L. Rev. 171 (1959); Note, 50 Yale L.J. 1286 (1941).

[312] A church divorce has no legal force. See Hilton v. Roylance, 25 Utah 129, 69 Pac. 660 (1902); Norton v. Tufts, 19 Utah 470, 57 Pac. 409 (1899).

[313] Goldens v. Arons, 36 N.J. Super. 371, 115 A.2d 639 (1955). Cf. Hughes v. Holman, 110 Ore. 415, 223 Pac. 730 (1924).

[314] Mertens v. Mertens, 38 Wash. 2d 55, 227 P.2d 724 (1951).

joined Jehovah's Witnesses, in the absence of overt acts of cruelty or harshness, was not grounds for divorce, since it is not an act of cruelty to change one's religion.[315]

Two disparate cases relating to the marriage relationship remain to be noted. In 1950, the highest court of Illinois held invalid a provision in a new divorce statute which authorized the master in chancery to summon a minister, priest or rabbi, or other religious representative, to a hearing at which reconciliation would be attempted.[316] The court ruled that this amounted to the utilization of a tax-supported instrumentality for the administration of justice to aid religious groups spread their faith. Similarly, a New York court has ruled invalid a section of a statute which provided that marriage may be solemnized only by clergymen who were duly ordained and affiliated with any religion listed in the last federal census of religious bodies.[317] Since cults which do not have distinctive memberships are not listed, the court held that the statute was an unwarranted legislative restriction upon the recognition of religious bodies, and thus an invasion of the constitutional guaranty of religious freedom. The court said that "it is more desirable by far to tolerate the abuses of a few charlatans than to give judicial approval and sanction to a legislative enactment patently repugnant to the principles of religious liberty."[318]

Religious Issues in Civil Courts. While the principle of the separation of church and state is an admonishment to the courts of the state not to get involved in matters of religious belief or ecclesiastical polity, as such, nevertheless there are many situations, especially where property rights are involved, where the courts cannot or will not refuse to take jurisdiction.[319] A good example is a recent Michigan case involving a dispute between two factions of an Orthodox synagogue.[320] The congregation was founded in 1911, and in conformity with Orthodox Jewish custom, the women were seated in a separate balcony apart from the men. This eventually led to serious controversy, and in 1955 a majority of the congregation voted for mixed seating. Thereupon the embattled minority which wanted to continue the good old ways went to court asking for an injunction to restrain mixed seating. The trial court refused to take the case, but the Supreme Court of Michigan held that a civil court had jurisdiction to settle this dispute. While it agreed that

---

[315] Frantzen v. Frantzen, 349 S.W.2d 765 (Tex. Civ. App. 1961), noted in 2 J. Family Law 61 (1962); see also, Ryan v. Ryan, 114 S.W. 464 (Tex. Civ. App. 1908). Contra: Smith v. Smith, 61 Ariz. 373, 149 P.2d 683 (1944).
[316] People ex rel. Bernat v. Bicek, 405 Ill. 510, 91 N.E.2d 588 (1950).
[317] In re Saunders, 37 N.Y.S.2d 341 (Sup. Ct. 1942).
[318] Id. at 343.
[319] See Duesenberg, Jurisdiction of Civil Courts over Religious Issues, 20 Ohio St. L.J. 508 (1959); Pfeffer, Church, State, and Freedom, ch. 8 (1953).
[320] Davis v. Scher, 356 Mich. 291, 97 N.W.2d 137 (1959).

a civil court has no jurisdiction over ecclesiastical questions, and may not interfere with the practice of religion in any way, it held that it is proper to decide disputes over property. The court went on to state that it was established law in Michigan that the majority faction of a church congregation may not divert the property of the society, as against a faithful minority, to doctrines fundamentally opposed to the characteristic doctrines of the society. Many Michigan court decisions were cited in support of this proposition.

Of course, courts will not undertake to pass judgment on such purely religious matters as the proper administration of church sacraments,[321] but there are many aspects of church life where courts will take jurisdiction. Courts have accepted suits brought by individuals for reinstatement of membership,[322] and suits filed for reinstatement of a pastor,[323] or for the payment of contracted salary,[324] or to prevent a discharged pastor from continuing to conduct services.[325] Courts have been willing to decide cases involving the right of a church to buy and sell property,[326] the right of a church group to compel rental of a privately-owned auditorium,[327] burial rights,[328] and the granting of corporate charters.[329] Above all, courts will decide a dispute between two groups of members of a church, each of which claims to be the proper board of trustees.[330] For example, where there has been a fire in a church, and two different groups of members claim the insurance as the proper governing board of the church, then a civil court must step in to decide which group is entitled to the money.[331]

It is a familiar fact of church history that occasionally congregations break up into competing factions. Their theological differences are no

---

321 Carter v. Papineau, 222 Mass. 464, 111 N.E. 358 (1916).
322 Randolph v. First Baptist Church, 53 Ohio Op. 288, 120 N.E.2d 485 (1954), noted in 3 St. Louis L.J. 304 (1955); Galton v. Nesson, 201 Mass. 534, 88 N.E. 2 (1909); Jones v. State, 28 Neb. 495, 44 N.W. 658 (1890); Hendryx v. People's United Church, 42 Wash. 336, 84 Pac. 1123 (1906). See Fellman, The Constitutional Right of Association 36-38 (1963). Contra, Mt. Olive Primitive Baptist Church v. Patrick, 252 Ala. 672, 42 So. 2d 617 (1949); Stewart v. Jarriel, 206 Ga. 855, 59 S.E.2d 368 (1950); Minton v. Leavell, 297 S.W. 615 (Tex. Civ. App. 1927).
323 King v. Smith, 106 Kan. 624, 189 Pac. 147 (1920); State ex rel. Hynes v. Holy Roman Apostolic Catholic Church, 183 Mo. App. 190, 170 S.W. 396 (1914); Rector, Church of Holy Trinity v. Melish, 3 N.Y.2d 476, 146 N.E.2d 685 (1957).
324 Fisher v. Congregation B'Nai Yitzhok, 177 Pa. Super. 359, 110 A.2d 881 (1955).
325 Parish of the Immaculate Conception v. Murphy, 89 Neb. 524, 131 N.W. 946 (1911); Collins v. Simms, 254 N.C. 148, 118 S.E.2d 402 (1961).
326 Mertz v. Schaeffer, 271 S.W.2d 238 (Mo. App. 1954), noted in 3 St. Louis L.J. 310 (1955); Stone v. Salt Lake City, 11 Utah 2d 196, 356 P.2d 631 (1960).
327 Savoy v. Graham Memorial Auditorium, 329 S.W.2d 352 (Tex. Ct. App. 1959).
328 McQuire v. St. Patrick's Cathedral, 54 Hun. 207, 7 N.Y.S. 345 (1889).
329 Application of Conversion Center, Inc., 388 Pa. 239, 130 A.2d 107 (1957).
330 Pentecostal Tabernacle of Muncie v. Pentecostal Tabernacle of Muncie, 128 Ind. App. 145, 146 N.E.2d 573 (1957).
331 Ibid.

concern of the state, and a civil court has no business undertaking to decide who is right and whose doctrine is erroneous. But if the dispute involves the question as to which competing group has a lawful right to occupy the church building, then the civil courts cannot remain aloof, since there may be no alternative to a court action in the resolution of a dispute over the right to occupy property. Such disputes have for centuries been grist for the mill of the civil courts. In all probability, the main concern of the very early common law courts in medieval England was precisely to adjudicate disputes over the occupancy and ownership of property. The state cannot very well sit by and permit contesting church groups to resort to violence to settle the issue, for again, the avoidance of the resort to violence as a method of settling disputes is one of the most elemental and essential functions of the state.

A civil court is almost invariably embarrassed to get involved in the theological niceties of religious schism, and while it must take jurisdiction, it generally seeks to hold its responsibilities to a bare minimum. Thus American courts follow two basic rules in this area. If the dispute is between factions of a locally self-governing congregational church, the majority prevails,[332] except that many decisions hold that a majority may not change the denominational affiliation of a church.[333] This means that normally, in suits between competing factions of a congregational church, the court limits its inquiry to determining which faction is the majority. The other rule is that in the case of hierarchical or centrally-organized churches, the court will follow the decision of the proper hierarchical or institutional authority.[334] In these situations the court's inquiry is limited to the determination of the decision of this authority.

The United States Supreme Court took this position in 1871, in the celebrated case of *Watson v. Jones*.[335] This litigation grew out of a squabble between the pro-slave and unionist factions of the Presbyterian Church of Louisville, Kentucky. The Court held that since the local congregation was a member of and under the control of a larger religious organization, it was bound by the decision of the general assembly -of that church, and a court was obliged to accept that decision as final

---

[332] Ragsdall v. Church of Christ in Eldora, 244 Iowa 474, 55 N.W.2d 539 (1952); Grantham v. Humphries, 185 Miss. 496, 188 So. 313 (1939); Murr v. Maxwell, 232 S.W.2d 219 (Mo. App. 1950); McGinnis v. Watson, 41 Pa. 9 (1861); see Comment, 54 Mich. L. Rev. 102 (1955).

[333] Reid v. Johnston, 241 N.C. 201, 85 S.E.2d 114 (1954); Kempf v. Lentz, 68 N.E.2d 339 (Ohio 1943).

[334] Trustees of E. Norway Lake N.E.L. Church v. Halvorson, 42 Minn. 503, 44 N.W. 663 (1890); Ohio Annual Conference v. Richards, 58 Ohio Op. 219, 130 N.E.2d 736 (1954); St. Vincent's Parish v. Murphy, 83 Neb. 630, 120 N.W. 187 (1909).

[335] 80 U.S. (13 Wall.) 679 (1871); see, Chafee, The Internal Affairs of Associations Not for Profit, 43 Harv. L. Rev. 993 (1930); Comment, 43 Calif. L. Rev. 322 (1955).

and binding. Justice Miller pointed out that on complicated theological questions the judges of the civil courts were not as competent as the ecclesiastical judicatories to make decisions. Furthermore, it was not proper, he said, in a country devoted to religious freedom and the separation of church and state, for the civil courts to make independent judgments on matters of faith. Said Justice Miller:

> In this country the full and free right to entertain any religious belief, to practice any religious principle, and to teach any religious doctrine which does not violate the laws of morality and property, and which does not infringe personal rights, is conceded by all. The law knows no heresy, and is committed to the support of no dogma, the establishment of no sect. The right to organize voluntary religious associations to assist in the expression and dissemination of any religious doctrine, and to create tribunals for the decision of controverted questions of faith within the association, and for the ecclesiastical government of all individual members, congregations, and officers within the general association, is unquestioned.[336]

In 1952, in the important *Kedroff* decision,[337] the Supreme Court reaffirmed the position it took in *Watson v. Jones*. At issue in *Kedroff* was the right to occupy and use the St. Nicholas Cathedral of the Russian Orthodox Church, located in New York. The contest was between the appointee of the Patriarch of Moscow, the supreme authority of this church, and the head of an American faction whose claim to the Cathedral rested upon a statute enacted by the Legislature of New York in 1945. The Court held that the decision of the central hierarchical authority of the Church was entitled to enforcement, and that a state statute which purports to decide which group is the right and proper group to control the Cathedral was in conflict with the constitutional guaranty of the free exercise of religion and the separation of church and state. Speaking for the Court, Justice Reed leaned heavily upon *Watson v. Jones*, pointing out that the opinion in that case "radiates . . . a spirit of freedom for religious organizations, an independence from secular control or manipulation—in short, power to decide for themselves, free from state interference, matters of church government as well as those of faith and doctrine."[338]

In a concurring opinion Justice Frankfurter emphasized that courts have jurisdiction to settle controversies over property, but only in strict subordination to the ecclesiastical law of the particular church. "Legislatures," he wrote, "have no such obligation to adjudicate and no such

---

[336] 80 U.S. (13 Wall.) at 728-29; see also Trustees of Presbytery v. Westminster Presbyterian Church, 222 N.Y. 305, 118 N.E. 800 (1918).
[337] Kedroff v. St. Nicholas Cathedral, 344 U.S. 94 (1952), noted in 34 B.U.L. Rev. 110 (1954), 54 Colum. L. Rev. 435 (1954), 2 J. Pub. Law 191 (1953), 28 Notre Dame Law. 398 (1953), 102 U. Pa. L. Rev. 405 (1954).
[338] 344 U.S. at 116.

power. Assuredly they have none to settle conflicts of religious authority and none to define religious obedience."[339] He rejected the argument that New York may protect itself from dangers attributed to the submission of the mother church in Moscow to the authority of a communist government. He noted that this would involve the state in the business of assessing the foreign political entanglements of many churches. ". . . Under our Constitution," Justice Frankfurter asserted, "it is not open to the governments of this Union to reinforce the loyalty of their citizens by deciding who is the true exponent of their religion."[340]

The Supreme Court remanded the *Kedroff* case to the New York Court of Appeals, which proceeded to reach on common law grounds the same conclusion it had arrived at earlier. The Supreme Court reversed again, pointing out that it is of no constitutional significance that the state acted this time solely through its judicial branch, for whether the state acts through its legislature or through its courts, it is still being asked to scrutinize an application of state power.[341]

Thus, in the very act of reasserting the principle of the separation of church and state, courts are involved in the affairs of the church, if only to give effect to decisions made by appropriate church authority. The civil courts cannot remain aloof, because they are committed to settling disputes over property. That the disputants in a particular case are factions of a church does not mean that the courts cannot take jurisdiction, though the search for a settlement is conditioned by church law and practice.

Other Court Pronouncements on Religion. There are innumerable situations where the judges of the civil courts get involved in assessing the religiousness of religious institutions. To cite a very simple illustration of a problem which has been litigated only in the recent past, prisoners in our penitentiaries are entitled to practice their religion. The question has arisen: are the Black Muslims a religious group within the meaning of prison rules or statutes on the subject? Founded in Detroit in 1930 by an American Negro who calls himself Muhammad Elijah, it is said to have 100,000 members, and preaches black supremacy and the complete separation of the races.[342] It has all the trappings of a religion: a holy book (a version of the Koran), priests, temples, schools, dietary laws, and taboos, and it enforces a strict sex morality. In addition, some wardens have found the Black Muslim inmates hard

---

[339] Id. at 122.
[340] Id. at 125. Dissenting alone, Justice Jackson argued that New York was not obliged, by anything in the constitution, to "yield to the authority of a foreign and unfriendly state masquerading as a spiritual institution." Id. at 131.
[341] Kreshik v. St. Nicholas Cathedral, 363 U.S. 190 (1960), noted in 35 N.Y.U.L. Rev. 1370 (1960), 32 Miss. L.J. 118 (1960).
[342] See Comment, 62 Colum. L. Rev. 1488 (1962) ; Lincoln, The Black Muslims in America (1961).

to handle, and have therefore denied them the opportunity to practice whatever they call their religion on the ground that it is not really a religion. The Court of Appeals of the Second Circuit, however, ruled in 1961 that the Black Muslims are a religion within the meaning of the Constitution.[343] The Court of Appeals for the Fourth Circuit held, in the same year, that the trial court erred in refusing to entertain a complaint without a hearing on the ground of lack of jurisdiction over matters of prison discipline and conduct.[344] Pointing out that a prisoner does not forfeit all of his civil rights, the court held that under the Civil Rights Act of 1871[345] a court may grant injunctive relief under these circumstances.

The Supreme Court of California resolved this problem differently in ruling on a petition for habeas corpus filed by ten Black Muslim inmates of the state prison at Folsom requesting court aid to prevent interference with their practice of their religion.[346] Having had a great deal of trouble with the Muslims, the warden would not permit them to purchase their Koran. In resisting the petition for habeas corpus, the Director of Corrections of California took the position that these Muslims were not a religious group or sect. The supreme court affirmed a denial of the writ, holding that even if it is conceded that the Muslims are a religious group, under the circumstances the decision of the warden was not unreasonable, in view of the inflammatory character of Muslim doctrine. The court ruled that while prisoners may not be punished solely because of their Muslim beliefs, the prison officials may enforce proper rules and maintain order. Reasonable censorship of printed matter in the hands of inmates is a necessary element of prison administration, and not a denial of fundamental rights. The United States Supreme Court made this decision final by denying certiorari.[347] Similarly a New York court ruled, also in 1961, that prison officials could refuse to permit a Black Muslim to take an Arabic grammar into the prison yard.[348] The court held that, assuming this was the practice of religion, prison officials could restrict its use to places other than the prison yard. This is a matter of discipline to be decided by the prison officials rather than by the courts. Finally, a New Jersey court ruled in 1957 that it was not an interference with a Catholic prisoner's reli-

---

[343] Pierce v. LaVallee, 293 F.2d 233 (2d Cir. 1961), noted in 24 Ga. B.J. 519 (1962), 75 Harv. L. Rev. 837 (1962) ; see also Comment, 35 So. Cal. L. Rev. 162 (1962).

[344] Sewell v. Pegelow, 291 F.2d 196 (4th Cir. 1961).

[345] Rev. Stat. § 1979 (1875), 42 U.S.C. § 1983 (1958).

[346] In re Ferguson, 55 Cal. 2d 663, 361 P.2d 417 (1961), noted in 28 Brooklyn L. Rev. 330 (1962), 9 U.C.L.A.L. Rev. 501 (1962).

[347] 368 U.S. 864 (1961).

[348] People ex parte Wright v. Wilkins, 26 Misc. 2d 1090, 210 N.Y.S.2d 309 (1961).

gious freedom to keep him in solitary confinement, where he was being punished for unruly and troublesome conduct, and thus prevent him from attending Mass on Sunday and holy days with the other Catholic prisoners.[349] The freedom to practice religion, the court said, must be considered in the light of the state's social interest in the preservation of order and discipline in the prison. This particular prisoner, it was asserted, should be "privileged to worship God to the extent that his conduct in prison permits."

Another illustration of the seemingly inevitable involvement of civil courts with religious matters is found in such a simple situation as prosecution for the offense of disturbing religious worship. Many states have criminal laws of this sort. In a prosecution under such a statute, however, if the accused offers as a defense the contention that the meeting he is alleged to have disturbed was not in fact a religious meeting within the meaning of the statute, then the court must make a decision on the point. Thus on one occasion a man was convicted of disturbing a Christmas tree celebration on Christmas eve in a public school building which was used as both a schoolhouse and a church-house.[350] In upholding the conviction the Oklahoma court declared that the term "religious worship" can have "no technical meaning in a legal sense, and is not restricted to any denomination, sect, or mode of religious worship. In its true sense a religious meeting is an assemblage of people met for the purpose of performing acts of adoration to the Supreme Being, or to perform religious services in recognition of God as an object of worship, love, and obedience, it matters not the faith with respect to the Deity entertained by the persons so assembled."[351]

Furthermore, almost all of the states permit the incorporation of religious organizations, and again, in construing such statutes a court may be called upon to decide whether a particular group qualifies under the law. Thus in a widely-noted decision the Iowa Supreme Court once had occasion to rule that the then communistic Amana society was entitled to the privilege of incorporation as a religious organization even though it owned and managed property.[352] The court declared that it could not very well say that a scheme of life designed to remove the temptations to rapacity and ambition which are nurtured by contests for wealth did not pertain to religion. The court said: "When theologians formulate their conclusion that anything such as a particular mode of life is essential to the attainment of the promised benefits of a religion, it is not for the courts by resorting to the definitions of

---

[349] McBride v. McCorkle, 44 N.J. Super. 468, 130 A.2d 881 (1957).
[350] Cline v. State, 9 Okla. Crim. 40, 130 Pac. 510 (1913).
[351] Id. at 44, 130 Pac. at 512.
[352] State v. Amana Soc'y, 132 Iowa 304, 109 N.W. 894 (1906).

lexicographers to perform the ungracious, if not herculean, task of determining whether this is so."[353]

Blasphemy was a crime at the common law, and some fourteen states still have statutes making blasphemy a crime.[354] In enforcing these statutes—and prosecutions are now extremely rare—courts in this country have had to skate on pretty thin ice. In a leading decision of the Massachusetts court rendered in 1838, Chief Justice Shaw declared that since the only purpose of blasphemy laws was "to restrain and punish acts which have a tendency to disturb the public peace,"[355] they do not violate the constitutional guaranties of freedom of speech and religion. He defined blasphemy as speech having "an intended design to calumniate and disparage the Supreme Being, and to destroy the veneration due to him," but he was careful to point out that "it does not prohibit the fullest inquiry, and the freest discussion, for all honest and fair purposes, one of which is the discovery of truth." Furthermore, "it does not prevent the simple and sincere avowal of a disbelief in the existence and attributes of a supreme, intelligent being, upon suitable and proper occasions." Even so, the Supreme Court of the United States ruled, in 1952, that a New York statute which banned the showing of motion picture films on the statutory ground that they are "sacrilegious" violated the constitutional guaranty of free speech.[356] The New York Court of Appeals had construed the statutory provision to mean "simply this," that: "no religion, as that word is understood by the ordinary, reasonable person, shall be treated with contempt, mockery, scorn and ridicule."[357] The statute as thus defined, Justice Clark said, "is far from the kind of narrow exception to freedom of expression which a state may carve out to satisfy the adverse demands of other interests of society." He added that under this statute "the censor is set adrift upon a boundless sea amid a myriad of conflicting currents of religious views, with no charts but those provided by the most vocal and powerful orthodoxies."[358] Furthermore, said Justice Clark, "the state has no legitimate interest in protecting any or all religions from views distasteful to them which is sufficient to justify prior restraints upon the expression of those views. It is not the business of government in our nation to suppress real or imagined attacks upon a particular religious doctrine,

---

[353] Id. at 314-15, 109 N.W. at 898.

[354] See Pfeffer, op. cit. supra note 319, at 543-47.

[355] Commonwealth v. Kneeland, 37 Mass. (20 Pick.) 206, 220 (1838). See also the opinion of Chancellor Kent in People v. Ruggles, 8 Johnson R. 290 (N.Y. 1811). For a more recent decision leaning heavily on the Kneeland case, see State v. Mockus, 120 Me. 84, 113 Atl. 39 (1921).

[356] Joseph Burstyn, Inc. v. Wilson, 343 U.S. 495 (1952).

[357] Joseph Burstyn, Inc. v. Wilson, 303 N.Y. 242, 258, 101 N.E.2d 665, 672 (1951).

[358] Joseph Burstyn, Inc. v. Wilson, 343 U.S. 495, 504-05 (1952).

whether they appear in publications, speeches, or motion pictures."[359] There has been no criminal prosecution for blasphemy in any state for a good many years, and it is most dubious that it could be reconciled with this decision.

Finally, the courts are involved in all sorts of religious matters in dealing with cases relating to the creation of religious trusts. For example, they may be called upon to decide whether the terms prescribed in a bequest are unenforceable as against public policy. Thus, in the famous *Girard* case,[360] decided by a unanimous Court in 1844, a bequest of a large sum of money to be held in trust for a college in Philadelphia was upheld even though it had been stipulated that no "ecclesiastic, missionary, or minister of any sect" should ever be permitted to teach there, or even enter the premises as a visitor. The will was attacked by heirs of the deceased on the ground that it was hostile to the Christian religion and therefore void as against the common law and public policy of Pennsylvania. The Court upheld the will on the theory that it did not say that Christianity shall not be taught in the school, but simply barred ecclesiastics. It was pointed out that laymen may also instruct in the general principles of Christianity. While Justice Story agreed that the Christian religion could be regarded as part of the common law of Pennsylvania, this proposition had to be understood as qualified by the constitutional guaranty of complete religious freedom.

Similarly, in 1880, a will was contested in the Pennsylvania courts on the ground that the trust which it created in behalf of a library required it to publish books periodically which denied the truth of the Christian religion.[361] The court said: "It may be regarded as settled in Pennsylvania, that a court of equity will not enforce a trust where its object is the propagation of atheism, infidelity, immorality or hostility to the existing form of government. A man may do many things while living which the law will not do for him after he is dead. He may deny the existence of a God, and employ his fortune in the dissemination of infidel views, but should he leave his fortune in trust for such purposes, the law will strike down the trust as *contra bonos mores*."[362]

It is, of course, universally recognized that religious gifts are public charities.[363] It has been said that "care for the poor, sympathy for the afflicted, and efforts to elevate mankind are but expressions and manifestations of religion."[364] There is a great deal of evidence that since

---

[359] Id. at 505.
[360] Vidal v. Girard's Ex'rs, 43 U.S. (2 How.) 127 (1844).
[361] Manners v. Philadelphia Library Co., 93 Pa. 165 (1880).
[362] Id. at 172.
[363] See McNeilly v. First Presbyterian Church, 243 Mass. 331, 137 N.E. 691 (1923); Strother v. Barrow, 246 Mo. 241, 151 S.W. 960 (1912); Humphreys v. State, 70 Ohio St. 67, 70 N.E. 957 (1904); Zollmann, American Law of Charities ch. 5 (1924).
[364] City of San Antonio v. Salvation Army, 127 S.W. 860, 862 (Tex. Civ. App. 1910).

the eighteenth century courts have enforced trusts for religion as charities.[365] Where religious trusts are very indefinite, they are usually
enforced as trusts for such religion as the trustee selects,[366] though some
have been held unenforceable because they are too vague or uncertain.[367]
Equity courts will enforce any trust as charitable which promotes any
principles of any organization which can actually be regarded as religious, and, as a famous Massachusetts judge once said, "in this
country since the Revolution no distinction has been made between
charitable gifts for the benefit of different religious sects."[368] But this
inevitably leads the courts to consider, in contested and marginal cases,
what a religion is, or whether a particular association or activity is in
fact a religious purpose. Thus courts have upheld bequests to a society
of Quakers,[369] to a group engaged in "Fire Baptized Holiness work,"[370]
to a "Christ Doctrine Revealed and Astronomical Science Association,"[371] to Mormon groups,[372] to Christian Science churches,[373] to the
Salvation Army,[374] to a Shaker group,[375] to a Unitarian Society,[376] and
to a Friendship Liberal League which held Sunday meetings devoted to
moral improvement.[377] Thus the Kentucky court, in holding that a
Shaker group cannot be regarded as committed to superstitious uses,
pointed out that "by our constitution, all religions are viewed as equally
orthodox."[378] In view of the recognition which religion generally has
attained from common consent and legislative enactments, the court
held that it must regard every religious use as a pious use, and so long
as piety is highly prized, the law must encourage it.

---

[365] See 2A Bogert, Trusts and Trustees § 375 (1953).
[366] Attorney Gen. v. Wallace's Divisees, 46 Ky. (7 Monroe) 611 (1847);
Rhodes v. Yater, 27 N.M. 489, 202 Pac. 698 (1922); In re Thompson's Estate,
282 Pa. 30, 127 Atl. 446 (1925).
[367] Bridges v. Pleasants, 39 N.C. 26 (1845).
[368] Gray, J., in Jackson v. Phillips, 96 Mass. (14 Allen) 539, 554 (1867).
[369] Kelly v. Nichols, 18 R.I. 62, 25 Atl. 840 (1892).
[370] Leak's Heirs v. Leak's Ex'r, 25 Ky. L. Rep. 1703, 78 S.W. 471 (1904).
[371] In re Budd, 166 Cal. 286, 291, 135 Pac. 1131, 1134 (1913).
[372] Staines v. Burton, 17 Utah 331, 53 Pac. 1015 (1898); Richtman v. Watson,
150 Wis. 385, 136 N.W. 797 (1912).
[373] Chase v. Dickey, 212 Mass. 555, 99 N.E. 410 (1912); Glover v. Baker,
76 N.H. 393, 83 Atl. 916 (1912).
[374] In re Crawford's Estate, 148 Iowa 60, 126 N.W. 774 (1910); Lane v.
Eaton, 69 Minn. 141, 71 N.W. 1031 (1897); Salvation Army v. American Salvation Army, 120 N.Y.S. 471, 135 App. Div. 268 (1909), appeal withdrawn, 200
N.Y. 555, 93 N.E. 1131 (1909).
[375] Gass v. Wilhite, 32 Ky. (2 Dana) 170 (1834).
[376] In re Hinckley, 58 Cal. 457, 512 (1881). The court said that as applied to
moral questions, religion involves "only a recognition of a conscientious duty to
recall and obey restraining principles of conduct."
[377] In re Knight's Estate, 159 Pa. 500, 28 Atl. 303 (1894). Said the court: "It
is not necessary to fix with precision the views, the practices, or the influence of
this body of men and women. It is enough to know that the league is in effect
their church; and that its services are intended to give expression to their peculiar
views about religion, and in some way to aid in the social, intellectual and moral
elevation of themselves and others." Id. at 504, 28 Atl. at 304.
[378] Gass v. Wilhite, 32 Ky. (2 Dana) 170, 176 (1834).

But there have been cases where, in concrete situations, a particular use or purpose was held to be outside the scope of the concept of religion; adoption by parties of a religious tag is by no means conclusive upon the courts. Thus a gift for the purpose of promoting spiritualism through the upkeep of a memorial at a camp has been held void, as contrary to the rule against perpetuities, because it was not devoted to any religious use.[379] A federal court once held that a theosophical society, which lacked a coherent and organized membership, but which was found to be "merely a voluntary association of a few persons," was not a religion.[380] Furthermore, a trust for the support of discussion under the auspices of an infidel society has been held not to be charitable in character.[381] A leading scholar on trusts has written: "Whether any American court would declare charitable a trust to spread atheistic or infidelistic ideas by lectures, discussions, or books may be strongly doubted. While theoretically the truth should prevail, and it should be for the public welfare that all questions be open for discussion and critical consideration, practically it seems probable that the belief in some form of religion, however simple, is so deeply rooted in the American public, that a trust to attack religion would be regarded as antisocial and apt to lead to the degradation of mankind rather than to its elevation or improvement."[382]

Furthermore, many early cases hold that when a fund is created by a religious society for education in its faith, the fund cannot be diverted from its original object, and if this is done a court of equity will give a remedy.[383] "In such case," a court has observed, "the question is not which faith or doctrine is the soundest or most orthodox; this is not the object of the enquiry, but for what object or purpose was the fund originally established by the founders of it?"[384] And, as a New York judge once noted, "the exercise of jurisdiction . . . in cases of this kind, is not without its difficulties."[385] In addition, in deciding whether a charity is for a religious purpose, the courts have found it necessary to rule on such ancillary matters as the propriety of gifts for the support of clergymen, or for the maintenance of a parsonage, or for the retire-

---

[379] In re Stephan's Estate, 129 Pa. Super. 396, 195 Atl. 653 (1937).

[380] Korsstrom v. Barnes, 167 Fed. 216 (W.D. Wash. 1909). A gift to further the "broadest interpretation of metaphysical thought" was upheld in Vineland Trust Co. v. Westendorf, 86 N.J. Eq. 343, 98 Atl. 314 (1916), aff'd, 87 N.J. Eq. 675, 103 Atl. 1054 (1916).

[381] Zeisweiss v. James, 63 Pa. 465 (1870).

[382] Bogert, op. cit. supra note 365, at 140-41.

[383] Ferraria v. Vanconcellos, 31 Ill. 25, 46 (1863); Hale v. Everett, 53 N.H. 9 (1868); Attorney Gen. v. Moore's Ex'rs, 19 N.J. Eq. (4 C.E. Green) 503 (1868); Robertson v. Bullions, 9 Barb. 64 (N.Y. Sup. Ct. 1850); Fadness v. Braunborg, 73 Wis. 257, 41 N.W. 84 (1889).

[384] Field v. Field, 9 Wend. 394, 401 (N.Y. 1832) (Nelson, J.).

[385] Gable v. Miller, 10 Paige 627, 646-47 (N.Y. Ch. 1844) (Chancellor Walworth).

ment of superannuated preachers, or for the support of Sunday or parochial schools, or the education of ministers, or missions, or masses.[386]

It would seem to follow, from this review of an assortment of different situations and problems, that while the concept of the separation of church and state is firmly rooted in American constitutional law and political thought, the affairs of the state and the affairs of religion intertwine at numerous points. Even when the state turns its friendliest face to religion it inevitably gets involved with religion. If churches are given the privilege of tax exemption, then the courts must decide, at least in the marginal situations, what a church is. When the state exempts from compulsory military service persons who are conscientious objectors on religious grounds, the civil courts must decide in specific cases whether particular claimants are sincerely what they claim to be. In many aspects of domestic relations, in the law of trusts and corporations, and in the general area of property law, the courts are inevitably and frequently involved in handling some aspects of controversies or problems which are essentially religious in character. That religion is involved is often a bar to a court's taking jurisdiction should not obscure the fact that very often the courts do take jurisdiction. They may be reluctant to do so, and they may suffer pangs of embarrassment, but in settling property disputes or ruling on tax exemptions or upon adoption and guardianship problems, the courts do the job that is expected of them.

V

Some of the most disputed issues relating to the constitutional relationships between church and state are now found in the field of education. There are, in fact, two different sets of issues. One is concerned with the legal propriety of appropriating public tax money for the aid of church schools. The other group of questions deals with the extent to which it is permissible to bring religion into the classrooms of the public schools. In both areas there are strong and widely shared commitments. Thus, the Committee on Education of the New York Constitutional Convention of 1894 declared that in its opinion "there is no demand from the people of the State upon this convention so unmistakable, widespread and urgent; none, moreover, so well grounded in right and reason, as that the public school system of the State will be forever protected by constitutional safeguards from all sectarian influence or interference, and that public money shall not be used, directly or indirectly, to propagate denominational tenets or doctrines."[387]

State aid to church schools has become a burning issue, and that it

---

386 Zollmann, op. cit. supra note 363, at 168-80.
387 New York Constitutional Convention of 1894, 4 Revised Record 861.

should be such is wholly understandable. On the one hand, the Supreme Court has taken a firm position on the proposition that there is a federally-protected constitutional right, under the due process clause of the fourteenth amendment, to maintain and to attend non-public church schools.[388] In holding a state statute unconstitutional which required all children to attend public schools between the ages of eight and sixteen, the Court declared that "the fundamental theory of liberty upon which all governments in this Union repose excludes any general power of the state to standardize its children by forcing them to accept instruction from public teachers only. The child is not the mere creature of the State; those who nurture him and direct his destiny have the right, coupled with the high duty, to recognize and prepare him for additional obligations."[389] At the same time, the Court had no doubt that the state has the power to require the private schools to observe reasonable regulations regarding school age, qualifications of teachers and curriculum.[390] Nevertheless, in several well-known decisions the Court has had occasion to indicate that government may not go too far, as in prohibiting the use of a foreign language[391] or pushing regulation to such a point as to amount to affirmative direction.[392] The courts will permit the states to go far in imposing regulations upon the public schools,[393] however, even to the point of forbidding the teaching of evolution.[394]

Not only is there a constitutional right to maintain and attend church schools, but some religions attach the highest importance to the maintenance of such schools. Thus a distinguished church scholar has written: "Catholics are morally obliged to secure a religious training for their children, and this does not mean religion separated from life, religion as a subject given during special and released time during the week or on Sundays, but religious truths in literature, in philosophy, in history, not to speak of other subjects."[395] According to the latest available figures of the United States Office of Education, there are today 91,853 public

---

[388] Pierce v. Society of Sisters, 268 U.S. 510 (1925). This statement was cited with approval by Justice Black in Everson v. Board of Educ., 330 U.S. 1, 18 (1947).
[389] 268 U.S. at 535.
[390] For a convenient survey of state statutes on this subject, see National Education Association Research Bulletin, Vol. 34, December 1956, The State and Sectarian Education, Ch. IV, State Supervision of Sectarian Education.
[391] Meyer v. Nebraska, 262 U.S. 390 (1923); Mo Hock Ke Lok Po v. Stainback, 74 F. Supp. 852 (D. Hawaii 1947), rev'd and remanded on procedural grounds, 336 U.S. 368 (1949).
[392] Farrington v. Tokushige, 273 U.S. 284 (1927).
[393] Berea College v. Kentucky, 211 U.S. 45 (1908).
[394] Scopes v. State, 154 Tenn. 105, 289 S.W. 363 (1927). See Keebler, Limitations upon the State's Control of Public Education, 6 Tenn. L. Rev. 153 (1928); Turck, State Control of Public School Curriculum, 15 Ky. L.J. 277 (1927); Note, 27 U. Chi. L. Rev. 505 (1960).
[395] Wise, Federal Aid for Religious Schools, 62 School & Society 363 (1945).

elementary schools with 27,601,902 pupils, 25,784 public secondary schools with 8,484,869 pupils, 13,574 private elementary schools with 4,639,696 pupils, and 4,061 private secondary schools with 1,035,247 pupils.[396] Obviously those who choose to support the private schools assume heavy financial obligations and ease the burden of the tax-supported schools. "No one conscious of religious values," Justice Rutledge once wrote, "can be unsympathetic toward the burden which our constitutional separation puts on parents who desire religious instruction mixed with secular for their children. They pay taxes for others' children's education, at the same time the added cost of instruction for their own. Nor can one happily see benefits denied to children which others receive, because in conscience they or their parents for them desire a different kind of training others do not demand."[397] Nevertheless, the great weight of American constitutional law is against the extension of public financial aid to the church schools. While federal expenditures cannot be challenged in the courts because the Supreme Court has ruled that a taxpayer, *qua* taxpayer, lacks standing to sue,[398] no such principle prevails in the jurisprudence of the states. Every state constitution but one has one or more provisions which can be construed as limiting or prohibiting the expenditure of public money for sectarian education, and these are judicially enforceable.[399]

In construing these provisions, the state courts have held a wide variety of direct aids to be illegal. They almost invariably rule that the granting of public money to parochial schools for general expenses of operation or to cover tuition costs are either in violation of some state constitutional restriction,[400] or do not come within the scope of statutes dealing with public school aids.[401] In a recent opinion on this subject

---

[396] See Statesman's Year-Book, 1963-1964, p. 591.

[397] Everson v. Board of Educ., 330 U.S. 1, 58 (1947) (dissenting opinion).

[398] Frothingham v. Mellon, 262 U.S. 447 (1923). For the application of this rule to religious matters, see Doremus v. Board of Educ., 342 U.S. 429 (1952), involving Bible-reading in the public schools, and Elliott v. White, 23 F.2d 997 (D.C. Cir. 1928), involving an unsuccessful attempt to enjoin the payment of salaries to chaplains in the armed forces and those serving Congress. See Jaffe, Standing to Secure Judicial Review: Public Actions, 74 Harv. L. Rev. 1265 (1961).

[399] See Note, 96 U. Pa. L. Rev. 230 (1947); Comment, Catholic Schools and Public Money, 50 Yale L.J. 917 (1941).

[400] Atchison, T. & S.F.R.R. v. Atchison, 47 Kan. 712, 28 Pac. 1000 (1892); Williams v. Stanton School Dist., 173 Ky. 708, 191 S.W. 507 (1917); Underwood v. Wood, 93 Ky. 177, 19 S.W. 405 (1892); In re Opinion of the Justices, 214 Mass. 599, 102 N.E. 464 (1913); Otken v. Lamkin, 56 Miss. 758 (1879); People ex rel. Roman Catholic Orphan Asylum Soc'y v. Board of Educ., 13 Barb. 400 (N.Y. 1851); Synod v. State, 2 S.D. 366, 50 N.W. 632 (1891); Almond v. Day, 197 Va. 419, 89 S.E.2d 851 (1955), noted in 42 Va. L. Rev. 437 (1956); Swart v. School Dist., 122 Vt. 177, 167 A.2d 514, cert. denied, 366 U.S. 925 (1961), noted in 29 Fordham L. Rev. 578 (1961).

[401] Berghorn v. Reorganized School Dist., 364 Mo. 121, 260 S.W.2d 573 (1953); Donoghue v. Smith, 119 Vt. 259, 126 A.2d 93 (1956). In State ex rel. Atwood v. Johnson, 170 Wis. 251, 176 N.W. 224 (1920), the court ruled that an

the highest court of Virginia brushed aside the child-benefit argument with the observation that "tuition and institutional fees go directly to the institution and are its very life blood."[402] And the Supreme Court of Vermont pointed out, in 1961, that "the same fundamental law which protects the liberty of a parent to reject the public system in the interests of his child's spiritual welfare, enjoins the state from participating in the religious education he has selected."[403] Furthermore, in a number of cases state courts have ruled that a school which purports to function as a public school, but which is in fact a religious school dominated or controlled by a church, is not entitled to state financial aid.[404]

On the other hand, the courts usually uphold the payment of public money to orphanages,[405] homes for delinquent children,[406] and hospitals, [407] even though they are operated by religious associations, generally on the ground that the state is merely paying for a benefit it would otherwise have to provide for directly. There have been, however, some contrary decisions.[408] The question of supplying textbooks to parochial school children has been litigated several times, and the courts are divided.[409] The Supreme Court of the United States has upheld the expenditure of tax funds for this purpose, by unanimous vote, but this was in 1930, before the due process clause had been permitted to absorb

---

educational bonus act for war veterans was not invalid because the recipient attends a religious institution. Cf. Reuben Quick Bear v. Leupp, 210 U.S. 50 (1908).

[402] Almond v. Day, 197 Va. 419, 427, 89 S.E.2d 851, 857 (1955).

[403] Swart v. School Dist., 122 Vt. 177, 188, 167 A.2d 514, 520 (1961).

[404] Knowlton v. Baumhover, 182 Iowa 691, 166 N.W. 202 (1918); Wright v. School Dist., 151 Kan. 485, 99 P.2d 737 (1940); Williams v. Stanton School Dist., 173 Ky. 708, 191 S.W. 507 (1917); Richter v. Cordes, 100 Mich. 278, 58 N.W. 1110 (1894); Harfst v. Hoegen, 349 Mo. 808, 163 S.W.2d 609 (1942); State ex rel. Public School No. 6 v. Taylor, 122 Neb. 454, 240 N.W. 573 (1932); Zellers v. Huff, 55 N.M. 501, 236 P.2d 949 (1951). Contra, State ex rel. Johnson v. Boyd, 217 Ind. 348, 28 N.E.2d 256 (1940).

[405] New Haven v. Torrington, 132 Conn. 194, 43 A.2d 455 (1945); Crain v. Walker, 222 Ky. 828, 2 S.W.2d 654 (1928); Sargent v. Board of Educ., 177 N.Y. 317, 69 N.E. 722 (1904); Murrow Indian Orphan's Home v. Childers, 197 Okla. 249, 171 P.2d 600 (1946).

[406] St. Hedwig's Industrial School for Girls v. Cook County, 289 Ill. 432, 124 N.E. 629 (1919); Dunn v. Chicago Industrial School, 280 Ill. 613, 117 N.E. 735 (1917); Schade v. Institution Dist., 386 Pa. 507, 126 A.2d 911 (1956), noted in 103 U. Pa. L. Rev. 440 (1953).

[407] Bradfield v. Roberts, 175 U.S. 291 (1899); Kentucky Bldg. Comm'n v. Effron, 310 Ky. 355, 220 S.W.2d 836 (1949); Craig v. Mercy Hospital, 209 Miss. 427, 45 So. 2d 809 (1950), noted in 22 Miss. L.J. 110 (1950); Opinion of the Justices, 99 N.H. 519, 113 A.2d 114 (1955).

[408] State ex rel. Nevada Orphan Asylum v. Hallock, 16 Nev. 373 (1882) (orphanages); Collins v. Kephart, 271 Pa. 428, 117 Atl. 440 (1921) (hospitals).

[409] In favor of free textbooks for parochial school children: Borden v. Louisiana, 168 La. 1005, 123 So. 655 (1929); Chance v. State Textbook R. & P. Bd., 190 Miss. 453, 200 So. 706 (1941). Contra, Donahoe v. Richards, 38 Me. 376 (1854); Dickman v. School Dist. No. 62 C, 223 Ore. 347, 366 P.2d 533 (1961), cert. denied sub nom. Carlson v. Dickman, 371 U.S. 823 (1962); Smith v. Donohue, 202 App. Div. 656, 195 N.Y.S. 715 (1922); Haas v. Independent School Dist., 69 S.D. 303, 9 N.W.2d 707 (1943).

the religious clauses of the first amendment.[410] The Court merely ruled, in rejecting due process objections, that the expenditure was for a public purpose. There are many other issues which relate to the general question of the propriety of various uses of public funds which have been the subject of litigation. Thus courts usually permit the construction of chapels at such public places as county poor farms and old age homes.[411] Many courts have taken the position that there is no legal impropriety in the hiring of nuns by school boards,[412] though on this point there is a minority view.[413] It is worth noting that all children who attend tax-exempt schools are entitled to the benefits of the National School Lunch Act,[414] and that the federal Hospital Survey and Construction Act extends to hospitals maintained by religious associations.[415] Under the "G.I." Bill of 1944, veterans could attend denominational schools to which payments were made directly.[416] Most states allow church groups to use public school buildings during off-hours,[417] and the courts generally sustain the practice on *de minimis* grounds.[418]

The debate over the constitutional propriety of spending public money to aid nonpublic schools is epitomized in the controversy over the legality of providing pupils with bus transportation to parochial schools at public expense. The Supreme Court ruled on this question for the first and only time, in 1947, in the *Everson* case,[419] in which, by a five-to-four vote, it was held that bus transportation did not violate the due process clause of the fourteenth amendment. But the issue had been litigated many times in the state courts prior to 1947, in terms of

---

[410] Cochran v. State Bd. of Educ., 281 U.S. 370 (1930).

[411] Bank of America Nat'l Trust & Sav. Ass'n v. Arakelian, 171 Cal. App. 732, 341 P.2d 61 (1959); Reichwald v. Catholic Bishop, 258 Ill. 44, 101 N.E. 266 (1913); Town of Pryor v. Williamson, 347 P.2d 204 (Okla. Sup. Ct. 1959). Cf. Koerner v. Borck, 100 So. 2d 398 (Fla. 1958).

[412] New Haven v. Torrington, 132 Conn. 194, 43 A.2d 455 (1945); Millard v. Board of Educ., 121 Ill. 297, 10 N.E. 669 (1887); State ex rel. Johnson v. Boyd, 217 Ind. 348, 28 N.E.2d 256 (1940); Rawlings v. Butler, 290 S.W.2d 801 (Ky. Ct. App. 1956); Gerhard v. Heid, 66 N.D. 267, 267 N.W. 127 (1936); Hysong v. School Dist., 164 Pa. 629, 30 Atl. 482 (1894); see Blum, Religious Liberty and the Religious Garb, 22 U. Chi. L. Rev. 875 (1955).

[413] Knowlton v. Baumhover, 182 Iowa 691, 166 N.W. 202 (1918); O'Connor v. Hendrick, 184 N.Y. 421, 77 N.E. 612 (1906); Commonwealth v. Herr, 229 Pa. 132, 78 Atl. 68 (1910). See Blum, supra note 413, at 888-95.

[414] 60 Stat. 230 (1946), 42 U.S.C. §§ 1753, 1760(d)(3) (1958).

[415] 60 Stat. 1013, 1015 (1946), 22 U.S.C. §§ 981(b), 1001(g) (1958).

[416] 58 Stat. 287, 290, § 400(11) (1944).

[417] See N.E.A. Research Bulletin, The State and Sectarian Education, p. 205.

[418] Southside Estates Baptist Church v. Board of Trustees, 115 So. 2d 697 (Fla. 1959); Nichols v. School Directors, 93 Ill. 61 (1879); Davis v. Boget, 50 Iowa 11 (1878); State v. Dilley, 95 Neb. 527, 145 N.W. 999 (1914); Lewis v. Board of Educ., 157 Misc. 520, 285 N.Y.S. 164 (Sup. Ct. 1935). Contra, Boyd v. Mitchell, 69 Ark. 202, 62 S.W. 61 (1901); Eckhardt v. Darby, 118 Mich. 199, 76 N.W. 761 (1898); State v. Board of Educ., 88 Ohio Op. 364, 100 N.E.2d 294 (1949), cert. denied, 340 U.S. 820 (1950); McKnight v. Board of Pub. Educ., 365 Pa. 422, 76 A.2d 207 (1950), appeal dismissed, 341 U.S. 913 (1951).

[419] Everson v. Board of Educ., 330 U.S. 1 (1947).

the provisions of the state constitutions dealing with church-state relations. These courts were sharply divided, though the weight of opinion was to the effect that this type of aid to religion was unconstitutional. The courts of Maryland, California, Kentucky and New Jersey took a position which was favorable to the transportation of children to non-public schools at public expense.[420] The Kentucky court held in 1942 that it was not legally proper to use public school funds for this purpose,[421] but it decided in 1946 that this rule did not apply to general county funds.[422] Speaking rather generally, these courts took the position that the expenditure of public funds for the purpose of transporting pupils to nonpublic schools did not constitute a use of such funds for private purposes, since the state is interested in seeing to it that all children of school age acquire an education by attending some school. The compulsory education law is complied with, of course, by going to a parochial school. Furthermore, these courts accepted the argument that bus transportation was for the benefit of the child, who is thus protected against the traffic hazards on the roads, and that the aid to the religious institution is only indirect or incidental, a mere "byproduct of proper legislative action."[423] They maintained that bus transportation was merely one of many social services which governments provide for all children, such as the maintenance of sidewalks and streets, police and fire protection. The objectives, "raising the standard of intelligence of youth and providing for the safety of children,"[424] are well within the scope of the police power.

On the other hand, prior to the *Everson* decision the courts of Delaware, Iowa, New York, Oklahoma, Pennsylvania, South Dakota, Washington and Wisconsin ruled that the transportation of children to nonpublic schools at public expense was illegal.[425] It should be noted,

[420] Bowker v. Baker, 73 Cal. App. 2d 653, 167 P.2d 256 (1946); Nichols v. Henry, 301 Ky. 434, 191 S.W.2d 930 (1946); Adams v. Commissioners, 180 Md. 550, 26 A.2d 377 (1942); Board of Educ. v. Wheat, 174 Md. 314, 199 Atl. 628 (1938); Everson v. Board of Educ., 133 N.J.L. 350, 44 A.2d 333 (1945).
[421] Sherrard v. Board of Educ., 294 Ky. 469, 171 S.W.2d 963 (1942).
[422] Nichols v. Henry, 301 Ky. 434, 191 S.W.2d 930 (1946).
[423] Board of Educ. v. Wheat, 174 Md. 314, 323, 199 Atl. 628, 632 (1938).
[424] Bowker v. Baker, 73 Cal. App. 2d 653, 663, 167 P.2d 256, 261 (4th Dist. 1946).
[425] State ex rel. Traub v. Brown, 36 Del. 181, 172 Atl. 835 (Sup. Ct. 1934), writ of error dismissed on the ground that the issue was moot, 39 Del. 187, 197 Atl. 478 (1938); School Dist. v. Parker, 238 Iowa 984, 29 N.W.2d 214 (1947); Judd v. Board of Educ., 278 N.Y. 200, 15 N.E.2d 576 (1938); Gurney v. Ferguson, 190 Okla. 254, 122 P.2d 1002 (1942); Connell v. School Directors, 356 Pa. 585, 52 A.2d 645 (1947); Hlebanja v. Brewe, 58 S.D. 351, 236 N.W. 296 (1931); Mitchell v. School Dist. No. 21, 17 Wash. 2d 61, 135 P.2d 79 (1943); Costigan v. Hall, 249 Wis. 94, 23 N.W.2d 495 (1946); State ex rel. Van Straten v. Milquet, 180 Wis. 109, 192 N.W. 392 (1923). It should be noted, however, that in Oklahoma Ry. v. St. Joseph's Parochial School, 33 Okla. 755, 127 Pac. 1087 (1912), the Oklahoma court ruled that under a franchise requiring reduced rates for all "school children" attending the "public schools," a railroad was obliged to offer reduced fares to

however, that the Pennsylvania, Iowa, South Dakota and Wisconsin cases were decided on non-constitutional, statutory grounds. They merely held that the statutes under which the school boards had acted did not empower them to provide transportation to parochial schools. Furthermore, the 1938 decision of the New York Court of Appeals was set aside by a constitutional amendment adopted in the same year which authorized the legislature to "provide for the transportation of children to and from any school or institution of learning."[426] An attempt was made in November, 1946, to overrule the Wisconsin decision by constitutional amendment, but the people voted it down.[427]

The cases which turned on the construction of state constitutional provisions rejected the child benefit theory and accepted the argument that free transportation of pupils attending sectarian schools would aid the schools. Thus the Oklahoma court characterized the child benefit theory as "not impressive," since "it is no less true that practically every proper expenditure for school purposes aids the child."[428] It said that the child benefit argument could be advanced with equal cogency to support the expenditure of public funds for the erection of school buildings, the payment of teachers' salaries, and the like. The court warned that transportation, if permitted, would open the door to other aids, and that this, in turn, would inevitably lead to state regulation or control of the parochial schools. Furthermore, the Supreme Court of Washington maintained that transportation would be illegal even if it did not entail any additional expense, though it concluded that some additional expense was in fact involved.[429] The New York Court of Appeals declared that children have a right to go to parochial schools, "but their attendance upon the parochial school or private school is a matter of choice and the cost thereof not a matter of public concern."[430] It added that "any contribution directly or indirectly made in aid of the maintenance and support of any private or sectarian school out of public funds would be a violation of the concept of complete separation of Church and State in civil affairs and of the spirit and mandate of our fundamental law."[431] The argument that furnishing transportation to pupils of nonpublic schools aided the pupils and not the schools the New York court characterized as "utterly without substance." It is

---

children attending parochial schools, under the doctrine that franchises must be strictly construed.

[426] N.Y. Const. art. XI, § 4.

[427] Wisconsin Blue Book 227 (1948). The vote was 437,817 for the amendment, and 545,475 against it.

[428] Gurney v. Ferguson, 190 Okla. 254, 255, 122 P.2d 1002, 1004 (1942).

[429] Mitchell v. Consolidated School Dist. No. 21, 17 Wash. 2d 61, 135 P.2d 79 (1943).

[430] Judd v. Board of Educ., 278 N.Y. 200, 211, 15 N.E.2d 576, 582 (1938).

[431] Ibid.

important to note that the provision of the New York constitution on which this decision turned forbade the expenditure of any public money which would be used, "directly or indirectly," to aid any school "wholly or in part under the control or direction of any religious denomination, or in which any denominational tenet or doctrine is taught."[432] The court had no doubt that transportation conferred at least indirect aid to the parochial schools. "Without pupils," it said, "there could be no school."[433]

The state cases which went against bus transportation on statutory grounds were decided by unanimous votes, but in the cases turning on constitutional issues the judges were sharply divided. Thus the New York case was decided by a four-to-three vote, and Chief Justice Crane filed a vigorous dissenting opinion. The Washington case was decided by a five-to-four vote, the dissenters drawing a distinction between direct aids and support and indirect aids or benefits, which the state constitution did not explicitly forbid. One judge dissented in the Oklahoma case. Furthermore, in the Maryland case which upheld the validity of this type of state aid the judges were divided five-to-three.

This issue finally reached the Supreme Court of the United States in the *Everson* litigation, and by a five-to-four vote transportation was upheld over fourteenth amendment due process objections. Certiorari proceedings had been brought by a taxpayer in a New Jersey trial court to set aside a school board's appropriation of money to reimburse Catholic parents for the cost of transporting their children to parochial schools.[434] A statute adopted by the state legislature in 1941 specifically authorized the school board to provide for transportation to any non-public school not operated for profit.[435] Dividing two-to-one, the court decided that the legislation extended state aid to sectarian private schools in violation of the state constitution. The New Jersey Court of Errors and Appeals, as it was then called, reversed the lower court by a six-to-three vote, holding that transportation enables parents to satisfy a duty imposed upon them by the compulsory education laws.[436] This being a matter of great public concern, the challenged expenditure is not for a private purpose. The minority specifically rejected the child benefit argument, pointing out that once this is conceded there is no logical stopping point. The dissenting opinion described the child benefit theory as "an ingenious effort to escape constitutional limitations rather than a sound construction of their content and purpose."[437] This opinion

[432] N.Y. Const. art. IX, § 4.
[433] 278 N.Y. at 212, 15 N.E.2d at 582.
[434] Everson v. Board of Educ., 132 N.J.L. 98, 39 A.2d 75 (Sup. Ct. 1944).
[435] N.J. Stat. Ann. § 18:14-8 (Supp. 1963).
[436] Everson v. Board of Educ., 133 N.J.L. 350, 44 A.2d 333 (1945).
[437] Id. at 362, 44 A.2d at 340.

78

also stressed the close connection between the parochial school and the church, from which it followed that the support of one was necessarily a support of the other.

The United States Supreme Court, by a five-to-four vote, affirmed the decision of the highest court of New Jersey.[438] The only federal issue was whether the state statute violated the due process clause of the fourteenth amendment, and the Court rejected the two due process contentions which had been advanced. First it held that the challenged expenditure of public funds was for a public and not a private purpose, pointing out that on this issue the Court has usually gone along with the combined judgment of the state lawmaking and judicial bodies.[439] Justice Black said that clearly facilitating the educational process by getting children to school safely was for a public purpose. Justice Black had more difficulty with the second issue, whether the expenditure in question violated the constitutional prohibition against the establishment of religion by law. Although he described the separation of church and state concept in very sweeping terms, and said that the wall of separation between them "must be kept high and impregnable," and that the Court cannot approve of "the slightest breach,"[440] he concluded that while the challenged statute approached "the verge" of the state's constitutional power, it was not invalid. Since the guaranty of the free exercise of religion ·commands that New Jersey may not hinder its citizens in the free exercise of religion, it follows, said Justice Black, that no individuals, "because of their faith or lack of it," can be excluded from receiving the benefits of public welfare legislation.[441] While he conceded that possibly some parents might have to send their children to public schools if not helped by the state to get them to church schools, he ruled that transportation aids are similar to other general governmental services, such as "ordinary police and fire protection, connections for sewage disposal, public highways and sidewalks."[442] Justice Black conceded that cutting off these services would make it more difficult for the religious schools to operate, but, he declared, that while the first amendment requires the state to be neutral in its relations with groups of believers and non-believers, "it does not require the state to be their adversary. State power is no more to be used so as to handicap religions than it is to favor them."[443] Parents have a legal right to satisfy the compulsory education laws by sending their children

---

[438] Everson v. Board of Educ., 330 U.S. 1 (1947).
[439] Id. at 6, citing Thompson v. Consolidated Gas Util. Corp., 300 U.S. 55 (1937) ; Green v. Frazier, 253 U.S. 233 (1920) ; Parkersburg v. Brown, 106 U.S. 487 (1882) ; Loan Ass'n v. Topeka, 87 U.S. (20 Wall.) 655 (1874).
[440] 330 U.S. at 18.
[441] Id. at 16.
[442] Id. at 17-18.
[443] Id. at 18.

to church schools, said Justice Black, and all New Jersey has done is provide "a general program to help parents get their children, regardless of their religion, safely and expeditiously to and from accredited schools."[444]

In his dissenting opinion Justice Jackson emphasized that the Catholic Church attached great importance to early and indelible religious indoctrination in the parochial schools. Since he thought that the parochial school was "a vital, if not the most vital, part of the Roman Catholic Church,"[445] a proposition which he doubted any Catholic would deny, it followed, in his view, that a subsidy of the sort under discussion was necessarily a subsidy to religion. He declared: "Catholic education is the rock on which the whole structure rests, and to render tax aid to its Church school is indistinguishable to me from rendering the same aid to the Church itself."[446] In a lengthy dissenting opinion, Justice Rutledge developed the thesis, from an historical point of view, that the broadly-phrased first amendment was intended to forbid not merely an established church, but any law respecting an establishment of religion. It was designed not merely to prohibit the official establishment of a single religion, he maintained, but "to create a complete and permanent separation of the spheres of religious activity and civil authority by comprehensively forbidding every form of public aid or support for religion. . . . The prohibition broadly forbids state support, financial or other, of religion in any guise, form or degree. It outlaws all use of public funds for religious purposes."[447] Justice Rutledge thought that the New Jersey tax aided children substantially to get religious training and teaching, and that transportation was not less essential than buildings, equipment, libraries, textbooks, and teachers.

The *Everson* decision was greeted by a storm of criticism. Those who favored state aid for religious schools objected to the first half of Justice Black's opinion, with its sweeping commitment to a "high and impregnable" wall of separation between church and state, and to the historical analysis set out in the dissenting opinion of Justice Rutledge.[448] The child benefit rationalization was applauded by many as a sensible gloss upon the relevant constitutional provisions.[449] On the other hand, many writers in the law reviews were very critical of the

---

[444] Ibid.
[445] Id. at 24.
[446] Ibid.
[447] Id. at 31-33.
[448] See O'Neill, Religion and Education under the Constitution ch. 11 (1949); Parsons, The First Freedom chs. 3-6 (1948); Schmidt, Religious Liberty and the Supreme Court of the United States, 17 Fordham L. Rev. 173 (1948); Note, 32 Marq. L. Rev. 138 (1948).
[449] See Blum, Religious Liberty and Bus Transportation, 30 Notre Dame Law. 384 (1955); Burke, Busses, Released Time and the Political Process, 32 Marq. L. Rev. 179 (1948); Note, 21 St. John's L. Rev. 176 (1947).

Court's decision, taking the position that the holding would serve as a justification for further state aids to religion.[450] "That the aid is to the pupil and therefore not to the school," one writer asserted, "is a clumsy, fictional means of circumventing the constitutional language."[451] Professor Thomas Reed Powell of the Harvard Law School asked: "How can it be proper for the public to pay for transport to religious instruction and worship from Monday through Friday if it could not provide free rides to Sunday or Saturday worship?"[452] The *New York Times* remarked editorially that it was both "reasonable and proper" for the state to use public funds for the direct benefit of a school child's health or safety, no matter what kind of school he attends.[453] On the other hand, an editorial in the *Washington Post* declared that "if citizens can be taxed to pay this expense, they can be taxed to pay the salaries of school teachers and the cost of buildings for religious education purposes. When and if this happens, the dominant group in any community will be in a position to dip into the public purse to propagate its own faith and the separation of church and state, as we have known it, will be nothing but a myth."[454] A prominent Baptist minister said: "This ominous decision casts a shadow, now no larger than a man's hand, but portending a cloud that may be drifting over every hamlet and dale from Plymouth Rock to the Golden Gate to darken the torch of religious liberty in our beloved land."[455] The Council of Bishops of the Methodist Church characterized the decision as a "departure from the American principle of the separation of church and state. . . ."[456] On the other hand, the editor of the *Louisville Courier-Journal* was "pleased to know that children are made safe from the hazards of traffic and weather because facilities will be available to them. . . ."[457]

So the debate ran when *Everson* was decided in 1947. It must be remembered, however, that all the Supreme Court decided in the *Everson* case was that a state expenditure of tax funds to transport pupils to parochial schools did not violate the fourteenth amendment to the

---

[450] See Note, 33 Cornell L.Q. 122 (1947) ; Note, 60 Harv. L. Rev. 793 (1947) ; Note, 22 N.Y.U.L.Q. Rev. 331 (1947) ; Note, 21 So. Cal. L. Rev. 61 (1947) ; Note, 33 Va. L. Rev. 349 (1947).
[451] Note, 96 U. Pa. L. Rev. 230 (1947).
[452] Powell, Public Rides to Private Schools, 17 Harv. Educ. Rev. 73 (1947).
[453] New York Times, July 26, 1949, p. 26.
[454] Washington Post, Feb. 13, 1947, quoted by Blanshard, American Freedom and Catholic Power 91 (1949).
[455] Dr. Louis D. Norton, in the New York Times, May 8, 1947, p. 22.
[456] New York Times, May 8, 1947, p. 26. See also Christian Science Monitor, Feb. 12, 1947, p. 14: The separation of church and state is a "bulwark of religious liberty. This decision . . . has torn down a whole section of that bulwark." For similar editorial opinion, see St. Louis Post-Dispatch, Feb. 13, 1947; Atlanta Constitution, Feb. 13, 1947; Chicago Tribune, Feb. 13, 1947, p. 18; 64 Christian Century 227 (1947).
[457] Louisville Courier-Journal, Feb. 11, 1947, p. 6. See also McSorley, 165 Catholic World 131 (1947).

81

United States Constitution. It did not and could not rule on the question as to whether such expenditure violates a provision of a state constitution. The highest court of a state determines with finality, so far as federal courts are concerned, what the state constitution means. A state court is at liberty to construe language in a state constitution differently from the way the United States Supreme Court construes identical language in the federal constitution. Furthermore, in *Everson* all the Court decided was that there is nothing in the federal constitution which forbids a state to provide free bus rides to church schools; it did not—and could not—decide that a state must do so. Though state courts are normally inclined to give great weight to the jurisprudence of the nation's highest appellate court, they are under no obligation to do so.

This is clearly shown by the state cases which have been decided since 1947. The only state courts to render a decision favorable to bus transportation for parochial school students since *Everson* was decided were those of Massachusetts and Connecticut. In 1955 the Massachusetts court ruled, without discussing any constitutional issues, that a town school committee is required by statute to provide such transportation.[458] The Supreme Court of Connecticut ruled, in 1960, that while money from the school fund could not constitutionally be spent for bus transportation, expenditures from the town general fund were valid as a proper police power measure serving the public health, safety and welfare.[459] On the other hand, the highest courts of Pennsylvania and Maine ruled, in 1956 and 1959 respectively, against bus transportation without discussing constitutional issues, merely holding that school districts lacked statutory authority to provide transportation.[460] Most significantly, however, the highest courts of five states have ruled squarely against the validity of bus transportation in terms of state constitutional provisions, since *Everson*.

The Supreme Court of Washington first ruled against bus transportation in 1943.[461] Reviewing the problem in 1949, it came to the same conclusion, holding that it could not follow *Everson's* lead because of the clear provisions in the state constitution forbidding the support of any religious establishment with public funds.[462] It characterized

---

[458] Quinn v. School Comm., 332 Mass. 410, 125 N.E.2d 410 (1955).
[459] Snyder v. Town of Newtown, 147 Conn. 374, 161 A.2d 770 (1960), appeal dismissed, 365 U.S. 299 (1961), noted in 35 Conn. B.J. 119 (March 1961). For an interesting account of the controversy over the bus question in Connecticut, see Powell, The School Bus Law (1960).
[460] Squires v. City of Augusta, 155 Me. 151, 153 A.2d 80 (1959); School Dist. v. Houghton, 387 Pa. 236, 128 A.2d 58 (1956). In the former case, the court said, per dictum, that if the legislature enacted such a statute, it would be constitutional, two judges dissenting at great length.
[461] Mitchell v. Consolidated School Dist. No. 201, 17 Wash. 2d 61, 135 P.2d 79 (1943).
[462] Visser v. School Dist. No. 506, 33 Wash. 2d 699, 209 P.2d 198 (1949) (two

transportation aid as "a direct, substantial, and continuing public subsidy to the schools, *as such* . . . ." The court held that in matters relating to religious instruction the state must be completely neutral, neither discouraging or encouraging religious schools by obstruction, on the one hand, or direct public subsidy, on the other. In 1953, the Supreme Court of Missouri ruled the same way, holding that bus transportation violated a section of the state constitution which provides that the state public school fund shall be used exclusively for the establishment and maintenance of the free public schools.[463] The highest court of Alaska ruled the same way, in 1961, on the basis of a provision in the state constitution forbidding the payment of public funds for the "direct benefit" of any religious educational institution.[464]

The Wisconsin Supreme Court ruled against bus transportation in 1923[465] and 1946,[466] both times by unanimous vote. A third case went the same way in 1962, though this time two judges dissented.[467] The court held that the challenged expenditure violated the provision in the state constitution which forbade the spending of public money "for the benefit of religious societies, or religious or theological seminaries." The court ruled that schools are seminaries, and that the authorizing statute benefitted them financially and increased their enrollments. The majority opinion gave approval to Professor Kurland's well-known statement: "The freedom and separation clauses should be read as stating a single precept: that government cannot utilize religion as a standard for action or inaction because these clauses, read together as they should be, prohibit classification in terms of religion either to confer a benefit or to impose a burden."[468] The child benefit rationale was rejected on the ground that it could be advanced with equal plausibility to justify any direct aid. The two dissenters accepted the child benefit theory and characterized the aid to the schools as only incidental.

Finally, in July, 1963, the Supreme Court of Oklahoma reaffirmed a

---

judges dissented), noted in 25 Notre Dame Law. 366 (1950), 25 N.Y.U.L. Rev. 410 (1950), 13 U. Det. L.J. 36 (1949), 11 U. Pitt. L. Rev. 318 (1950), 35 Va. L. Rev. 788 (1949).

[463] McVey v. Hawkins, 364 Mo. 44, 258 S.W.2d 927 (1953), noted in 3 St. Louis U.L.J. 273 (1955).

[464] Matthews v. Quinton, 362 P.2d 932 (Alaska 1961). The court divided two-to-one, the dissenter arguing that the aid in question was an indirect, and not a direct, benefit to the school.

[465] State ex rel. Van Straten v. Milquet, 180 Wis. 109, 192 N.W. 392 (1923).

[466] Costigan v. Hall, 249 Wis. 94, 23 N.W.2d 495 (1946). See Boyer, Public Transportation of Parochial School Pupils, 1952 Wis. L. Rev. 64; Setzler & Linford, A Constitutional Analysis of the Wisconsin School Bus Law, 1962 Wis. L. Rev. 500.

[467] State ex rel. Reynolds v. Nusbaum, 17 Wis. 2d 148, 115 N.W.2d 761 (1962). This case held Wis. Laws of 1961, ch. 648, unconstitutional.

[468] Kurland, Of Church and State and the Supreme Court, 29 U. Chi. L. Rev. 1, 96 (1961).

decision rendered in 1941[469] and ruled once more against bus transportation as a constitutionally forbidden appropriation of public money for the use, benefit or support, directly or indirectly, of any sect, church or system of religion.[470] The judges of this court were unanimous in holding that the law guarantees religious freedom, and if one wants to send his children to a parochial school, he must assume the financial burden which that choice entails. They felt that if buses aid the public schools, then if provided for the parochial schools, they also would be aided.

It is clear that the great weight of authority among the state courts is against bus transportation. Both before and after *Everson* most state courts have taken a position contrary to that of the United States Supreme Court. It is important to note, however, that all the Supreme Court has to go on is the vague due process clause of the fourteenth amendment. State constitutions, for the most part, are much more explicit and detailed on the subject of state aids to religion, and when a constitution provides that indirect as well as direct benefits to religion are forbidden, a state court does not have much room for maneuver. It would seem to follow that the legal means available in most states for the legitimizing of bus transportation to church schools at public expense is through constitutional amendment. Whether such an amendment is consistent with traditional American doctrine regarding the separation of church and state becomes a matter of judgment. Those who believe that bus transportation breaches the desired wall of separation often take the position that bus transportation helps the schools to which the pupils are brought, and that if this type of aid is proper, then they would not know how to make much of an argument against all other forms of assistance. Furthermore, they say that in the final analysis, if the state ever reaches the point of supporting the church schools generally, it will assume control as well. In that event, there would be only public schools. Accordingly, many doubt whether it would be possible to eat the cake of public aid and still retain the quality of private operation.

VI

The results of an extensive questionnaire survey, published in the spring of 1961, indicate that the religious influence is very pervasive

[469] Gurney v. Ferguson, 190 Okla. 254, 122 P.2d 1002 (1941).
[470] Board of Educ. v. Antone, 384 P.2d 911 (Okla. 1963). A study published in July, 1959, indicated that since Everson, to that date, 22 state Attorney-Generals ruled on bus transportation, with 13 contra, of whom seven went on constitutional grounds, six on statutory grounds. See Commission on Law and Social Action, American Jewish Congress, Digest and Analysis of State Attorney General Opinions Relating to Freedom of Religion and Separation of Church and State 52 (1959).

in American public schools.[471] Gideon Bibles were being distributed in 42.74 per cent of the school systems; baccalaureate services were a part of the graduation exercises of 86.84 per cent of the high schools; there were homeroom devotional services in 33.16 per cent of all schools of the school system, and in some of the schools of 17.06 per cent of the systems; there were regular chapel exercises in 22.07 per cent of the school systems (70.86 per cent in the South); there was Bible-reading in 41.74 per cent of the school systems (76.84 per cent in the South, 67.56 per cent in the East); Christmas was observed by activities in 87.92 per cent of the schools, and Easter by 57.82 per cent (Hannukah, 5.39 per cent, Passover, 2.17 per cent); 29.66 per cent of the school systems cooperated in programs of released time instruction, with 44.46 per cent in the East; 7.76 per cent of the public school classes were held in church buildings and members of religious orders were teaching in 5.76 per cent of the public schools.

Whether all of these activities can be reconciled with the principles set out in our national and state constitutions is one of the great areas of debate today. That so many activities which the courts regard as illegal persist suggests that obedience to law is not automatic in this country and far from universal. School boards, whether they are concerned with religion or race, have made a rich contribution to the American tradition of nullification. Perhaps the next anguished inquiry into the root causes of juvenile delinquency will take due note of this brand of adult delinquency in some of the American society's most respectable circles.

That the public schools must not invade the sphere of religious conscience of the pupils was underscored by the Supreme Court in 1943, when it decided that the compulsory flag salute could not lawfully be required of a student who objected to this sort of gesture on religious grounds.[472] When the Court was first confronted with this issue, in 1940, it upheld the compulsory flag salute, over the objections of a Jehovah's Witness child, on the ground that its purpose was the "promotion of national cohesion," which Justice Frankfurter characterized as "an interest inferior to none in the hierarchy of legal values," because "the ultimate foundation of a free society is the binding tie of cohesive sentiment."[473] He said that this issue should be determined by school boards and legislatures, and in the forum of public opinion, that the

---

[471] Dierenfield, The Extent of Religious Influence in American Public Schools, 56 Religious Education 173 (1961). The author sent out 4,000 questionnaires, of which 2,183 (54.57%) were returned. See also, N.E.A. Research Bulletin, The State and Sectarian Education 192-207; Punke, Religious Issues in American Public Education, 20 Law and Contemp. Prob. 138 (1955).
[472] West Virginia St. Bd. of Educ. v. Barnette, 319 U.S. 624 (1943).
[473] Minersville School Dist. v. Gobitis, 310 U.S. 586, 596 (1940).

courtroom was "not the arena for debating issues of educational policy," and that the Supreme Court was not "the school board for the country."[474] Justice Stone dissented alone, arguing that the government may not compel the affirmation of a belief which violates religious conviction, and that a compulsory expression of loyalty, exacted from an unwilling student, did not in fact promote national unity.

Some Justices quickly changed their minds, and in 1943, by a vote of six to three, the Court reversed the earlier decision.[475] After all, as Justice Frankfurter noted in the Court's opinion in the first case, we live by symbols, which means that symbols may well matter a great deal. A Biblical scholar has observed that "early Christian martyrdoms immediately come to mind. Often a slight gesture, little more than a flag salute, would have saved the martyrs, for their execution apparently was distasteful to Roman procurators and proconsuls. Polycarp of Smyrna was asked only to 'swear by the Good Fortune of Caesar.' Speratus, Donata, and the other Scillitan martyrs likewise were asked merely to swear by the *genius* of their lord, the emperor, and to pray for his safety. Speratus answered in words which Jehovah's Witnesses echo: 'I know no empire of this age, but rather I serve the God whom no one sees or can see.' "[476]

Speaking for the Court in the second flag salute case, Justice Jackson defined the issue at stake as whether it is legally permissible to compel students "to declare a belief," since clearly the flag salute and the accompanying pledge require the affirmation of a belief. He noted that it was not even alleged that a pupil who remains silent creates a clear and present danger of a serious evil, and that it would be quixotic to hold "that a Bill of Rights which guards the individual's right to speak his own mind, left it open to public authorities to compel him to utter what is not in his mind."[477] Government, he declared, has no power to coerce the acceptance of any patriotic creed, or to decree what shall be orthodox in politics, nationalism or religion. He also argued that the "compulsory unification of opinion achieves only the unanimity of the graveyard,"[478] that efforts to create unity by compulsion divide people rather than unify them. Justice Jackson refused to believe that the freedom to be spiritually and intellectually diverse would disintegrate the social order, and noted that "freedom to differ is not limited to

[474] Id. at 598.
[475] For a full account of the processes involved in the reversal, see the splendid account by Manwaring, Render Unto Caesar (1962).
[476] McCown, Conscience v. The State, 32 Calif. L. Rev. 1 (1944).
[477] West Virginia St. Bd. of Educ. v. Barnette, 319 U.S. 624, 634 (1943). In Lewis v. Allen, 5 Misc. 2d 68, 159 N.Y.S.2d 807 (1957), aff'd, 11 App. Dec. 2d 447, 207 N.Y.S.2d 862 (1960), a pledge of allegiance to "one nation, under God" was upheld, but it was carefully pointed out that reciting the pledge was voluntary.
[478] West Virginia St. Bd. of Educ. v. Barnette, supra note 477, at 641.

things that do not matter much. That would be a mere shadow of freedom. The test of its substance is the right to differ as to things that touch the heart of the existing order."[479] Justice Frankfurter wrote a lengthy and eloquent dissenting opinion in which he restated the position he had staked out when he spoke for the Court in the first flag salute case. He made a strong plea for judicial self-restraint, arguing that it was not a question of what he personally thought, but whether the state legislators could reasonably act as they did when they prescribed the compulsory flag salute and pledge. The constitutional guaranty of religious freedom, he insisted, did not create new privileges or new areas of civil immunity. The validity of secular laws in our society, he asserted, cannot be measured by their conformity to religious doctrines. This can happen only in a theocratic state.

The flag salute question involved an important issue of the individual's claim to religious freedom. But the first amendment, now applicable to the states through the fourteenth, forbids interference with religion by the state, on the one hand, and the establishment of religion by the state, on the other. An establishment of religion is constitutionally illicit, without regard to any question of coercion. This issue has been fought over most acutely in cases dealing with the legal propriety of including various forms of religious instruction or ceremony in the public school curriculum. The United States Supreme Court came to grips with one aspect of this problem in the *McCollum* case,[480] which was decided in 1948 with only one Justice dissenting. Mrs. McCollum, the mother of a child then enrolled in the public school of Champaign, Illinois, objected to the released time plan of religious education which the school board had adopted. Though she has been referred to as an "atheist," she has written that she was more aptly described as a "humanist," pointing out that the term "atheist" was too militant, and implied that she was a more profound student of theology than she really was.[481]

Under the released time plan to which Mrs. McCollum objected, religious instruction was given for a period of thirty or forty-five minutes each week, in the school building, during regular school time, to those children whose parents agreed by signing printed cards. The religious instruction was sectarian and given, at no expense to the school board, by religious teachers who came in from the outside. The children were taught in three separate religious groups by Protestant teachers, Catholic priests and a Jewish rabbi. Those students who did not choose to take the religious instruction were required to leave their classrooms and go to some other place in the school building, and continue with their

[479] Id. at 642.
[480] Illinois ex rel. McCollum v. Board of Educ., 333 U.S. 203 (1948).
[481] McCollum, One Woman's Fight 11 (1951).

secular studies. The trial court ruled that this dismissed time plan was legally unobjectionable, and by unanimous vote the Supreme Court of Illinois agreed.[482] The Supreme Court of the United States reversed, holding that beyond any question, the Champaign released time plan constituted "a utilization of the tax-established and tax-supported public school system to aid religious groups to spread their faith."[483] This, said Justice Black, falls squarely under the ban of the no-establishment clause of the first amendment. The Court specifically rejected the argument which counsel had advanced that historically the first amendment was intended to forbid only governmental preference of one religion over another, and not impartial government assistance to all religions. Justice Black denied that to hold that a state may not utilize its public school system to aid any or all religions manifested any governmental hostility to religion. "For the First Amendment," he wrote, "rests upon the premise that both religion and government can best work to achieve their lofty aims if each is left free from the other within its respective sphere."[484] The "wall of separation between Church and State," said Justice Black, is breached where the state uses the tax-supported public school buildings, and helps supply the pupils through use of the compulsory public school machinery, for the dissemination of religious doctrines.

In a long concurring opinion Justice Frankfurter emphasized how important the secular public school was for a democratic society, where children could be educated "in an atmosphere free from pressures in a realm in which pressures are most resisted and where conflicts are most bitterly engendered. Designed to serve as perhaps the most powerful agency for promoting cohesion among a heterogenous democratic people, the public school must keep scrupulously free from entanglement in the strife of sects."[485] Justice Frankfurter thought that the alternative offered to the child of not participating was not a decisive fact, because "the law of imitation operates, and non-conformity is not an outstanding characteristic of children."[486] Perhaps it is not inappropriate to

---

[482] People ex rel. McCollum v. Board of Educ., 396 Ill. 14, 71 N.E.2d 161 (1947). The Illinois court had previously ruled against compulsory Bible-reading, hymn-singing and praying in the public schools, People ex rel. Ring v. Board of Educ., 245 Ill. 334, 92 N.E. 251 (1910), but this case was distinguished on the ground that under the Champaign plan participation was voluntary, the plan was not part of the public school program, and all expenses were borne by the religious organizations. The court leaned heavily on People ex rel. Latimer v. Board of Educ., 394 Ill. 228, 68 N.E.2d 305 (1946), which had sustained the constitutionality of a dismissed time plan in use in Chicago.

[483] Illinois ex rel. McCollum v. Board of Educ., 333 U.S. 203, 210 (1951).

[484] Id. at 212.

[485] Id. at 216-17.

[486] Id. at 227. This is an important point, though not well developed. In some of the Bible-reading cases, state judges have called attention to the weakness in the argument that pupils are free to withdraw during the reading. See, e.g., State

observe that neither is non-conformity an outstanding characteristic of adults. Thus Justice Frankfurter concluded that the released time plan had the unhappy result of sharpening the consciousness of religious differences. Dissenting alone, Justice Reed took the position that while "aid" to any or all religions is not permissible, "aid" meant "a purposeful assistance directly to the church itself," but did not include "those incidental advantages that religious bodies, with other groups similarly situated, obtain as a by-product of organized society."[487] This principle, said Justice Reed, explains such practices as tax-exemption for churches, bus transportation to parochial schools, free textbooks and free lunches for their pupils. The no-establishment clause, he insisted, did "not bar every friendly gesture between church and state."[488]

Few cases in American history stirred up a greater storm of controversy than that which greeted the *McCollum* decision. Four cardinals and ten bishops published a statement through the Administrative Board of the National Catholic Welfare Council denouncing this decision as a victory for "doctrinaire secularism," and as an "entirely novel and ominously extensive" interpretation of the first amendment which paid "scant attention to logic, history, or accepted norms of legal interpretation."[489] The distinguished constitutional law scholar, Professor Edward S. Corwin of Princeton argued that the Court was guilty of bad history and faulty logic, maintaining that the establishment clause merely prohibits the national government from setting up an official church or from preferring one religion over another.[490] He insisted that the fourteenth amendment protects only "liberty," and he could not see how anyone's liberty had been invaded by the plan under discussion. The *McCollum* decision was criticized for setting up what was characterized as too absolutistic a rule, and as tending to undermine parental rights

---

ex rel. Weiss v. District Bd., 76 Wis. 177, 200, 44 N.W. 967, 975 (1890) : "The excluded pupil loses caste with his fellows, and is liable to be regarded with aversion, and subjected to reproach and insult." Kaplan v. School Dist., 171 Minn. 142, 155, 214 N.W. 18, 23 (1927) : "To excuse some children is a distinct preference in favor of those who remain and is a discrimination against those who retire. The exclusion puts a child in a class by himself. It makes him religiously conspicuous. It subjects him to religious stigma. It may provoke odious epithets. His situation calls for courage." (dissenting opinion). See also Knowlton v. Baumhover, 182 Iowa 691, 166 N.W. 202 (1918) ; Herold v. Parish Bd., 136 La. 1034, 68 So. 116 (1915).

[487] 333 U.S. at 248-49. For an exhaustive description of Justice Reed's views see O'Brien, Justice Reed and the First Amendment 107-98 (1958).

[488] 333 U.S. at 256.

[489] New York Times, Nov. 21, 1948.

[490] The Supreme Court as National School Board, 14 Law & Contemp. Prob. 3 (1949). In support, Corwin cited Story, Commentaries on the Constitution §§ 1874, 1879 (1833) ; Cooley, Constitutional Limitations 469 (2d ed. 1871), and Principles of Constitutional Law 224-25 (3d ed. 1898) ; see also O'Neill, Religion and Education under the Constitution ch. 12 (1959) ; Owen, The McCollum Case, 22 Temp. L.Q. 159 (1948).

with regard to the education of their children.[491] It was argued that the decision went too far, and thus endangered many existing practices. As for Justice Frankfurter's argument about "pressures," it was maintained that the "supposed neutrality" of the public schools was itself a pressure, and that the sheer omission of religion from the curriculum was itself a pressure against religion.[492] Of course the McCollum decision had its defenders,[493] but the adverse criticism was loud and clear and almost without parallel in volume and intensity.

It was argued at the time that the reasoning of the *McCollum* opinion would require invalidation of other schoolroom religious practices, such as the New York dismissed time plan of religious instruction, or Bible-reading and the recitation of prayers.[494] On the other hand, Justice Frankfurter maintained, in his concurring opinion in *McCollum,* that the Court was concerned only with the released time plan in use in Champaign, and hinted that "dismissed time" might be legally acceptable.[495] The Court was quickly given an opportunity to rule on the dismissed time plan in the *Zorach* litigation, which came up through the New York courts.

The only serious difference between the released time plan, which had been ruled invalid in *McCollum,* and the dismissed time plan which was challenged in New York was that in the latter plan the children leave the school building and go to some church for religious instruction. The central points of similarity are that the churches are still using time made available by the compulsory education law of the state, and that the public school authorities cooperate rather extensively in the actual administration of the plans. Some sort of dismissed time program had been tested in state courts prior to the *Zorach* litigation, and had been upheld over constitutional objections in Illinois, in 1946,[496] in California in 1947,[497] in New York in 1927, and again in 1948 after *McCollum.*[498] In 1959, seven years after *Zorach,* the Supreme Court of Washington

---

[491] Murray, Law or Prepossessions, 14 Law & Contemp. Prob. 23 (1949).
[492] Id. at 39. See also Lassiter, The McCollum Decision and the Public School, 37 Ky. L.J. 402 (1949); Stout, The Establishment of Religion under the Constitution, 37 Ky. L.J. 220 (1949); Comment, 22 So. Cal. L. Rev. 423 (1949).
[493] See, e.g., Blanshard, American Freedom and Catholic Power ch. 4 (1950); Dawson, Separate Church and State Now (1948); Thayer, Religion in Public Education (1947); Konvitz, Separation of Church and State: The First Freedom, 14 Law & Contemp. Prob. 44 (1949); Oxnam, Church, State, and Schools, 168 The Nation 67 (1949); Pfeffer, Religion, Education and the Constitution, 8 Law. Guild Rev. 387 (1948).
[494] See Note, 49 Colum. L. Rev. 836 (1949); Note, 57 Yale L.J. 1114 (1948).
[495] 333 U.S. at 231. See Patric, The Impact of a Court Decision: Aftermath of the McCollum Case, 6 J. Pub. L. 455 (1957).
[496] People ex rel. Latimer v. Board of Educ., 394 Ill. 228, 68 N.E.2d 305 (1946).
[497] Gordon v. Board of Educ., 78 Cal. App. 2d 464, 178 P.2d 488 (1947).
[498] People ex rel. Lewis v. Graves, 245 N.Y. 195, 156 N.E. 663 (1927); Lewis v. Spaulding, 193 Misc. 66, 85 N.Y.S.2d 682 (Sup. Ct. 1948), appeal withdrawn, 299 N.Y. 564, 85 N.E.2d 791 (1949).

upheld a dismissed time plan, though it did so on condition that church people were not to be permitted to come into the classrooms to recruit students, and that the teachers were not to have any part in the recruitment process.[499]

The *Zorach* litigation was initiated in July, 1948, and the New York Supreme Court, Kings County, ruled that the dismissed time plan was valid.[500] Dividing three to two, largely over the issue as to whether *McCollum* was controlling, the Appellate Division affirmed,[501] and the New York Court of Appeals also affirmed, with one judge dissenting.[502] Dividing six to three, the United States Supreme Court affirmed, holding that the fact that the children left the school building to receive religious instruction elsewhere was decisive in supporting the conclusion that the *McCollum* case was not controlling.[503] *McCollum* was neither re-examined nor overruled; it was distinguished. Speaking in dissent, Justice Black took the position that the difference between *McCollum* and *Zorach* was not significant, the whole point being that New York was using the compulsory education laws to help the religious sects get students who are presumably too unenthusiastic to go unless moved to do so by the pressure of the state machinery. In effect, he asserted, the state was making religious sects the beneficiaries of its power to compel children to attend secular schools; where the state manipulates its compulsory education laws to help the religious sects get pupils, there is not a separation but a combination of church and state. Similarly, Justice Frankfurter, also dissenting, maintained that "there is all the difference in the world between letting the children out of school and letting some of them out of school into religious classes."[504] Similarly, Justice Jackson argued that the New York system was more effective than voluntary attendance after school hours because of the truant officer supplied by the state. The school, he said, serves "as a temporary jail for a pupil who will not go to Church."[505] He protested that his opposition to the dismissed time plan was not antireligious. "My evangelistic brethren," he wrote, "confuse an objection to compulsion with an objection to religion."[506] And he went on to warn

---

[499] Perry v. School Dist. No. 81, 54 Wash. 2d 886, 344 P.2d 1036 (1959), noted in 35 Wash. L. Rev. 143 (1960).
[500] Zorach v. Clauson, 198 Misc. 631, 99 N.Y.S.2d 339 (Sup. Ct. 1950).
[501] Zorach v. Clauson, 278 App. Div. 573, 102 N.Y.S.2d 27 (1951).
[502] Zorach v. Clauson, 303 N.Y. 161, 100 N.E.2d 463 (1951). Judge Froessel said: "It is thus clear beyond cavil that the Constitution does not demand that every friendly gesture between church and State shall be discountenanced. The so-called 'wall of separation' may be built so high and so broad as to impair both State and church, as we have come to know them." Id. at 172, 100 N.E.2d at 467.
[503] Zorach v. Clauson, 343 U.S. 306 (1952).
[504] Id. at 320.
[505] Id. at 324.
[506] Ibid.

that "the day that this country ceases to be free for irreligion it will cease to be free for religion—except for the sect that can win political power."[507] Justice Jackson insisted that *McCollum* was controlling, and that the distinction made by the Court majority was "trivial, almost to the point of cynicism."[508]

Justice Douglas denied that the New York plan involved any element of coercion. He argued that no one was forced to go to the religious classroom, and that there was no evidence in the record to support the conclusion that coercion was used by the school authorities, who were completely neutral in the matter. The weakness of this argument, as pointed out by the dissenters, was that the plaintiffs had not been allowed to try to prove coercion. The New York Court of Appeals had declined to grant a trial on this issue because the point had not been properly raised under state practice, and Justice Douglas ruled that this was an independent state ground not reviewable in a federal court. Justice Frankfurter maintained that issues raising federal claims cannot and should not be foreclosed by state rules of practice.

Speaking for the Court, Justice Douglas reaffirmed the proposition that not only does the first amendment require the separation of church and state, but that "the separation must be complete and unequivocal,"[509] with no exceptions permitted. But he went on to say: "The First Amendment, however, does not say that in every and all respects there shall be a separation of Church and State. Rather, it studiously defines the manner, the specific ways, in which there shall be no concert or union or dependency one on the other. That is the common sense of the matter. Otherwise the state and religion would be aliens to each other—hostile, suspicious, and even unfriendly."[510] He said that if that were so, police and fire protection could not be rendered to churches, and such practices as the utterance of prayers in legislative halls and courtroom oaths would be illegal. "We are a religious people," Justice Douglas said, "whose institutions presuppose a Supreme Being."[511] We guarantee freedom of worship, and government may not show partiality to any one group, but, he asserted, "when the state encourages religious instruction or cooperates with religious authorities by adjusting the schedules of public events to sectarian needs, it follows the best of our traditions. For it then respects the religious nature of our people and accommodates the public service to their spiritual needs. To hold that it may not would be to find in the Constitution a requirement that the government show a callous in-

---

507 Id. at 325.
508 Ibid.
509 Id. at 312.
510 Ibid.
511 Id. at 313.

difference to religious groups. That would be preferring those who believe in no religion over those who do believe."[512] Nothing, Justice Douglas asserted, requires the government to be hostile to religion, though it is equally clear that "government may not finance religious groups nor undertake religious instruction nor blend secular and sectarian education nor use secular institutions to force one or some religion on any person."[513] The government must be neutral among the sects, said Justice Douglas, and is forbidden to make a religious observance compulsory; but it may close its doors or suspend operations for those who want to go to a church for worship or instruction. That is all that happened in this instance.

Since the Court was determined neither to overrule nor re-examine its decision in *McCollum,* a crucial issue in the *Zorach* case was whether the two decisions could be reconciled. Viewed from this angle, it is difficult to avoid the conclusion that since the difference between the two sets of facts was quite minute, the explanation for the latter decision may well be a loss of nerve on the part of the Justices, who yielded to the fierce barrage of adverse criticism which the *McCollum* decision had engendered. It is no longer any secret that judges, like the rest of us mortals, are human, and love approval and seek to avoid the pain of strong disapproval. I suspect that psychology rather than logic will explain the reconciliation of *Zorach* with *McCollum.* Thus Justice Jackson said, in his dissenting opinion in *Zorach,* that "today's judgment will be more interesting to students of psychology and of the judicial processes than to students of constitutional law."[514] As a matter of fact, Justice Douglas, in later opinions, discounted much of what he said in *Zorach.* Thus, in 1959, he went out of his way to argue, in a concurring opinion, that he rejected the notion "that First Amendment rights are somehow not fully realized unless they are subsidized by the State."[515] Speaking in dissent, in 1961, Justice Douglas went much further to argue "that if a religious leaven is to be worked into the affairs of our people, it is to be done by individuals and groups, not by the Government."[516] And he went on to say: "The 'establishment' clause protects citizens . . . against any law which selects any religious custom, practice, or ritual, puts the force of government behind it, and fines, imprisons, or otherwise penalizes a person for not observing it."[517]

That the *Zorach* decision was not destined to remain the lodestar of

[512] Id. at 313-14.
[513] Id. at 314.
[514] Id. at 325.
[515] Cammarano v. United States, 358 U.S. 498, 515 (1959).
[516] McGowan v. Maryland, 366 U.S. 420, 563 (1961).
[517] Id. at 564. See Sorauf, Zorach v. Clauson: The Impact of a Supreme Court Decision, 53 Am. Pol. Sci. Rev. 777 (1959); Reed, Church-State and the Zorach Case, 27 Notre Dame Law. 529 (1952).

Supreme Court divination on this subject became abundantly clear in 1962, in the New York Regents' prayer case, *Engel v. Vitale*.[518] The facts of this case were simple enough. The Board of Regents of the University of the State of New York drafted a short, nondenominational prayer of twenty-two words, as follows: "Almighty God, we acknowledge our dependence upon Thee, and we beg Thy blessings upon us, our parents, our teachers and our country." Use of this prayer was discretionary with the local school boards. The board of education for the school district at New Hyde Park, a Long Island suburb of New York, adopted a rule requiring the daily recitation of this prayer. No pupil was compelled to join in the prayer over his or his parents' objection. It is worth noting that in its amicus brief the Board of Regents said that its purpose in preparing this prayer was to inculcate in school children "the belief in a Supreme Being."[519] The parents of ten pupils brought legal action in the state courts to stop the practice. The trial court upheld the school board, provided that it was made clear that students were free to abstain from participation.[520] The Appellate Division affirmed in a per curiam opinion, with one of the five judges filing a concurring opinion to argue that this particular prayer did not constitute religious teaching.[521] The New York Court of Appeals also affirmed, but two judges dissented.[522] The majority emphasized the absence of coercion, and made much of "the natural law beliefs on which the Republic was founded and which in turn presuppose an Omnipotent Being."[523] Speaking in dissent, Judge Dye said that "no one doubts for a moment that we are a religious people,"[524] but he indicated that one reason for this was the first amendment's protection of religious freedom. The dissenters rejected the Regents' prayer as "a form of State-sponsored religious education"[525] which is best left to the churches alone.

With only one Justice dissenting, the Supreme Court reversed the holding of the three New York courts.[526] Justice Black declared that by using the public school system to encourage the recitation of a prayer, New York has adopted a practice wholly inconsistent with the establishment clause. Undoubtedly, he ruled, this is a religious activity—

---

[518] 370 U.S. 421 (1962).
[519] Brief for the Board of Regents, . . . as Amicus Curiae, p. 15, Engel v. Vitale, 370 U.S. 421 (1962), quoted by Kurland, The Regents' Prayer Case: Full of Sound and Fury, Signifying . . . , 1962 Sup. Ct. Rev. 1, 5.
[520] Engel v. Vitale, 18 Misc. 2d 659, 191 N.Y.S.2d 453 (Sup. Ct. 1959).
[521] Engel v. Vitale, 11 App. Div. 2d 340, 206 N.Y.S.2d 183 (1960).
[522] Engel v. Vitale, 10 N.Y.2d 174, 176 N.E.2d 579, 218 N.Y.S.2d 659 (1961).
[523] Engel v. Vitale, supra note 522, at 181-82, 176 N.E.2d at 582, 218 N.Y.S.2d at 662.
[524] Id. at 185, 176 N.E.2d at 584, 218 N.Y.S.2d at 664.
[525] Id. at 189, 176 N.E.2d at 586, 218 N.Y.S.2d at 666.
[526] Justices Frankfurter and White did not participate.

"a solemn avowal of divine faith and supplication for the blessings of the Almighty"[527]—and this was conceded by all parties, including the state authorities, and was so determined by the trial judge. "We think," said Justice Black, "that the constitutional prohibition against laws respecting an establishment of religion must at least mean that in this country it is no part of the business of government to compose official prayers for any group of the American people to recite as a part of a religious program carried on by government."[528] Justice Black made the historical point that one of the reasons why many early colonists left England to find religious freedom in America was this very practice of establishing governmentally-composed prayers. They knew, he said, that one of the greatest dangers to individual freedom of worship was in the government giving the official stamp of approval to one particular kind of prayer or religious service. Under the first and fourteenth amendments, Justice Black declared, it is established that neither the state nor the federal government has the power "to prescribe by law any particular form of prayer which is to be used as an official prayer in carrying on any program of governmentally sponsored religious activity."[529] Finally the Court ruled that without doubt the New York prayer "officially establishes the religious beliefs embodied in the Regents' prayer."[530] Since the issue here was not religious freedom, but rather violation of the establishment clause, the Court held that the fact that students were free to remain silent or leave the room was immaterial. Equally irrelevant was the denominationally neutral character of the prayer. The short of the matter is that religion is too personal, too sacred, and too holy to be put in the hands of civil authorities. Establishment of religion, Justice Black maintained, is bad for both religion and the state.

Justice Douglas wrote a concurring opinion to which the Court's critics have given special attention, for he took the occasion to question the constitutionality of all sorts of governmentally-financed religious exercises, such as the use of chaplains in Congress and in the service academies. He did not believe that the New York Regents' prayer amounted to an establishment of religion, but he did maintain that the state's neutrality towards religion is compromised when a public official on the public payroll performs a religious exercise in a governmental institution. The prayer in question does not conform with the tenets of all sects, to say nothing of agnostics, and thus, said Justice Douglas, it inserts a divisive influence into the community. Finally, he took the occasion to say that the *Everson* case[531] had been decided wrongly.

---

[527] 370 U.S. at 424.
[528] Id. at 425.
[529] Id. at 430.
[530] Ibid.
[531] Everson v. Board of Educ., 330 U.S. 1 (1947).

Justice Stewart, dissenting alone, protested that New York had not interfered with the free exercise of anybody's religion, and he could not see how a religion is established by permitting those who so desire to say a prayer. He insisted that this had nothing to do with the religious history cited by the Court. What matters most, he said, are the religious traditions of our people, as reflected in countless practices of governmental institutions.

Engel v. Vitale promptly triggered a storm of furious controversy, although it tended to diminish after the opinion had been read and digested.[532] A Senator said that "somebody is tampering with America's soul."[533] A famous evangelist declared: "This is another step toward the secularization of the United States."[534] A Cardinal asserted that he was "shocked and frightened," and that the decision "strikes at the very heart of the Godly tradition in which America's children have for so long been raised."[535] A Southern Congressman said: "They put the Negroes in the schools, and now they've driven God out."[536] A weekly magazine of opinion declared that the decision had "a petty, nasty quality."[537] Another journal of opinion asserted that it was "a stupid decision . . . that spits in the face of our history. . . ."[538] A Protestant bishop said that with this decision the Court "has just deconsecrated the nation."[539] There were angry speeches in Congress, the members of which promptly introduced some fifty constitutional amendments to overturn the decision.[540] A distinguished professor of constitutional law at the Harvard Law School criticized the decision on *de minimis* grounds, since he thought that the Regents' prayer "seems a pretty small religious exercise to hold unconstitutional as an establishment. . . ."[541] He said that "the somewhat ponderous judicial apparatus of state and nation has relieved the New Hyde Park schools of a twenty-two word invocation more doctrinally flavorless than grace before a community chest luncheon."[542] He also thought that in the absence of coercion or a burden on the pocketbook the Court should have exercised self-restraint and should have refused to take the case because the complaining parties

---

[532] For an interesting account of how the newspapers handled the story of this case see Hachten, Journalism and the Prayer Decision, Fall 1962 Colum. Journ. Rev. 4.

[533] Senator Robert C. Byrd, New York Times, July 1, 1962, § 4, p. 9.

[534] Billy Graham, New York Times, July 1, 1962, § 4, p. 9.

[535] Cardinal Spellman, New York Times, July 1, 1962, § 4, p. 9.

[536] Representative George W. Andrews of Alabama, New York Times, July 1, 1962, § 4, p. 1.

[537] The National Review, July 17, 1962, p. 10.

[538] America, July 7, 1962, p. 456.

[539] Bishop James A. Pike, Reader's Digest, October, 1962, p. 79.

[540] See, e.g., 108 Cong. Rec. 10883-85, 10897-98, 11102-08 (daily ed. July 26-30, (1962).

[541] Sutherland, Establishment According to Engel, 76 Harv. L. Rev. 25, 38 (1962).

[542] Id. at 45.

lacked standing to sue. In addition, in his Leary Lecture, delivered at the University of Utah on February 27, 1963, the Dean of the Harvard Law School strongly took Justice Black to task for taking a position which he described as extreme, absolutist, literal and Fundamentalist, on the subject of the separation of church and state.[543] He asserted that it is a matter of historical fact that this is a Christian nation, and that it is "sheer invention" to say that the first amendment requires "that all trace of religion be kept out of any sort of public activity."[544] He also insisted that the school prayer question was the sort of issue which should be settled in each community on the local level, particularly since no element of compulsion was involved. He said that the Constitution rightly provided for religious toleration, but that this did not mean "religious sterility."[545]

On the other hand, the Regents' prayer decision had strong editorial support in responsible newspapers and religious journals.[546] The decision was defended as a proper application of what the Founding Fathers had in mind when they wrote and adopted the first amendment.[547] It was noted that the *Engel* decision was consistent with the precedents (except for *Zorach*), which add up to the prescription that in religious matters the government must hold to a position of neutrality.[548] It was also pointed out that the decision in *Engel* did not go nearly as far as its critics were claiming,[549] special attention being drawn to a footnote in which Justice Black said this: "There is of course nothing in the decision reached here that is inconsistent with the fact that school children and others are officially encouraged to express love for our country by reciting historical documents such as the Declaration of Independence which contains reference to the Deity or by singing officially espoused anthems which include the composer's professions of faith in a Supreme Being, or with the fact that there are many manifestations in our public life of belief in God. Such patriotic or ceremonial occasions bear no true resemblance to the unquestioned religious exercise that the State of New York has sponsored in this instance."[550] In addition, competent legal scholars have insisted that there was an element of compulsion in the *Engel* case taking the form

---

[543] Griswold, Absolute Is in the Dark, 8 Utah L. Rev. 167 (1963).
[544] Id. at 174.
[545] Id. at 176.
[546] See editorials in New York Times, June 27, 1962, p. 34, and in The Christian Century, July 4, 1962, p. 832.
[547] See Levy, School Prayers and the Founding Fathers, 34 Commentary 225 (1962); Butts, The American Tradition in Religion and Education (1950).
[548] Pfeffer, Court, Constitution and Prayer, 16 Rutgers L. Rev. 735 (1962).
[549] Kauper, Prayer, Public Schools and the Supreme Court, 61 Mich. L. Rev. 1031 (1963).
[550] 370 U.S. at 435 n.21.

of indirect coercion arising from the fear of what amounts to social ostracism.[551]

Finally, some writers in religious journals have taken the position that the Regents' well-laundered prayer was objectionable to religious people as well as to nonbelievers. Said one writer: "I would not want my own children to have hammered into them, day after day in routine repetition, so self-centered and nationalistic a prayer. It is the Regents' prayer, not the court's decision, which Billy Graham should have termed 'another step toward the secularization of the United States.' "[552] He added: "The nub of the issue is the nature of prayer. When prayer becomes a coerced routine, it no longer is genuine prayer." And he asked: "Do we want religiosity or do we want religion? Outward piety or commitment? Outward slogans and symbols, or deep inner response? Insincere prayer is worse than no prayer." Similarly, the Executive Director of the Department of Religious Liberty of the National Council of the Churches of Christ, Reverend Dean M. Kelley, suggested that "the entrenchment and enforcement of a thin, flat, pale lowest-common-denominator State Religion of faith-in-Faith" was not the way to go about lifting the moral level of the nation. The Synagogue Council of America declared that "prayer of 'common core' can only lead to a watering down of all that is spiritually meaningful in every religious faith." Robert Van Deusen of the National Lutheran Council asked: "What happens when children recite a prayer by rote morning after morning? Is it really meaningful to them, or does it tend to innoculate them against a deeper and more perceptive experience?"[553] A group of 132 professors of law and political science signed a statement that was submitted on November 7, 1962, to the Senate Judiciary Committee, which made the same argument: "It is not the Supreme Court's decision but the action of state authorities in sponsoring public school recitation of prayer that is truly hurtful to religion. It is unreal to expect that an appreciation of religious values can be communicated to our children by the rote recitation of formalized prayer in public school classrooms. Whatever is good and meaningful in prayer must inevitably be lost by its mechanical repetition in an atmosphere devoid of the religious spirit which only the home and church can provide." They went on to point out that the selection by the authorities of a prayer taken from the liturgy of one faith would obviously be unfair to children of other faiths. A non-

---

[551] See Choper, Religion in the Public Schools: A Proposed Constitutional Standard, 47 Minn. L. Rev. 329 (1963); Kauper, supra note 549, at 1061.

[552] Miller, True Piety and the Regents' Prayer, 79 Christian Century 934 (1962).

[553] These and many other quotations by religious writers were gathered together by the Anti-Defamation League of B'nai B'rith, in a pamphlet entitled, "Prayer in the Public Schools." (n.d.)

sectarian prayer, such as that of the New York Regents, "not only infringes upon the rights of those affiliated with no religious body, but it poses the danger of the establishment of a new, public school religion which, in seeking to be least offensive, will succeed only in being least meaningful, and yet most pervasive."

It was wholly predictable, after the decision in the New York prayer case, that the Supreme Court would rule that such religious exercises as reading from the Bible and recitation of the Lord's Prayer were constitutionally improper in the public schools. So the Court held in June, 1963, by a vote of eight to one, in the *Schempp* case.[554] It had had an opportunity to rule on this matter in 1952, in a New Jersey case, but it had dismissed the appeal on the technical ground of lack of standing to sue on the part of the plaintiffs without ruling on the merits at all.[555] A very large number of state appellate courts, however, had ruled on the Bible-reading issue, prior to 1963, for this has been an old and hotly-debated question all over the country.[556] It should be noted that no state constitution specifically forbids Bible reading, although some twelve state constitutions forbid sectarian instruction in the public schools. On the other hand, one constitution, that of Mississippi, states that the guaranty of religious freedom shall not be construed "to exclude the Holy Bible from use in any public school of this state."[557] The fact situations in the Bible-reading cases were not all alike; in some the mere reading of the Bible was involved; in others the recitation of the Lord's Prayer was part of the exercises; in a few instances religious hymns were also sung. In some cases participation by the students was compulsory; in others, it was voluntary, and students could be excused. But in a general way these may be described as cases involving the issue of Bible-reading in the public schools.

While the state courts, prior to 1963, were divided on the issue, clearly the weight of authority, measured merely in terms of numbers, was on the side of holding that Bible-reading did not offend the federal and state constitutions. The appellate courts of the following states took this position: Colorado,[558] Florida,[559] Georgia,[560] Iowa,[561] Kansas,[562]

---

[554] Abington School Dist. v. Schempp, 374 U.S. 203 (1963).

[555] Doremus v. Board of Educ., 342 U.S. 429 (1952).

[556] See Boles, The Bible, Religion, and the Public Schools (2d ed. 1963); Frommer, The Bible and the Public Schools (1963); Cushman, The Holy Bible and the Public Schools, 40 Cornell L.Q. 475 (1955); Harrison, The Bible, the Constitution and Public Education, 29 Tenn. L. Rev. 363 (1962); Trimble, Bible Reading in Public Schools, 9 Vand. L. Rev. 849 (1956). See also Walter, Religion and the State University (1958).

[557] Miss. Const. art. III, § 18.

[558] People ex rel. Vollmar v. Stanley, 81 Colo. 276, 255 Pac. 610 (1927).

[559] Chamberlin v. Board of Pub. Instruction, 17 Fla. Supp. 183 (Cir. Ct. 1961), aff'd, 143 So. 2d 21 (Fla. 1962), judgment vacated and case remanded, 374 U.S. 487 (1963).

[560] Wilkerson v. City of Rome, 152 Ga. 762, 110 S.E. 895 (1922).

Kentucky,[563] Maine,[564] Maryland,[565] Massachusetts,[566] Michigan,[567] Minnesota,[568] New Jersey,[569] New York,[570] Ohio,[571] Pennsylvania,[572] Tennessee,[573] and Texas.[574] Appellate courts in the following states decided against Bible-reading: Illinois,[575] Louisiana,[576] Nebraska,[577] South Dakota,[578] Washington,[579] and Wisconsin.[580] In addition a three-judge federal district court, sitting in the eastern district of Pennsylvania, ruled against Bible-reading in 1962.[581]

The state courts were reluctant to approve of compulsory Bible-reading, however, and the absence of compulsion almost invariably made it easier for the courts to reach favorable conclusions. Speaking generally, those judges who voted to uphold the legality of Bible-reading maintained that it did not interfere with any one's religious freedom, and that the practice was not an act of worship. They usually ruled that the Bible is not a sectarian book, and that because of its importance as history and literature it is impossible to exclude it from the school curriculum. "If all *religious* instruction were prohibited," the Colorado court once said, "no history could be taught . . . . Even religious

---

[561] Moore v. Monroe, 64 Iowa 367, 20 N.W. 475 (1884).
[562] Billard v. Board of Educ., 69 Kan. 53, 76 Pac. 422 (1904).
[563] Hackett v. Graded Dist., 120 Ky. 608, 87 S.W. 792 (1905).
[564] Donahoe v. Richards, 38 Me. 379 (1854).
[565] Murray v. Curlett, 228 Md. 239, 179 A.2d 698 (1962).
[566] Commonwealth v. Renfrew, 332 Mass. 492, 126 N.E.2d 109 (1955); Spiller v. Inhabitants of Woburn, 94 Mass. (12 Allen) 127 (1866); Commonwealth ex rel. Wall v. Cooke, 7 Am. Law Reg. 417 (Police Ct. Boston, Mass. 1859).
[567] Pfeiffer v. Board of Educ., 118 Mich. 560, 77 N.W. 250 (1898).
[568] Kaplan v. Independent School Dist., 171 Minn. 142, 214 N.W. 18 (1927).
[569] Doremus v. Board of Educ., 5 N.J. 435, 75 A.2d 880 (1950), appeal dismissed, 342 U.S. 429 (1952), noted in 64 Harv. L. Rev. 666 (1951).
[570] Lewis v. Board of Educ., 157 Misc. 520, 285 N.Y.S. 164 (Sup. Ct. 1935), aff'd, 247 App. Div. 106, 286 N.Y.S. 174 (1936), appeal dismissed, 276 N.Y. 490, 12 N.E.2d 172 (1937).
[571] Nessle v. Hum, 2 Ohio Dec. 60 (C.P. 1894). In 1873 the Supreme Court of Ohio ruled that the state constitution neither enjoined nor required Bible-reading in the public schools. Board of Educ. v. Minor, 23 Ohio St. 211 (1872).
[572] Stevenson v. Hanyon, 7 Pa. D. & C.R. 585 (1898); Hart v. Sharpsville Borough School Dist., 2 Lancet. L. Rev. 346 (Pa. Mercer Co. Ct. 1885).
[573] Carden v. Bland, 199 Tenn. 665, 288 S.W.2d 718 (1956), noted in 55 Mich. L. Rev. 715 (1957).
[574] Church v. Bullock, 104 Tex. 1, 109 S.W. 115 (1908).
[575] People ex rel. Ring v. Board of Educ., 245 Ill. 334, 92 N.E. 251 (1910).
[576] Herold v. Parish Bd. of School Directors, 136 La. 1034, 68 So. 116 (1915).
[577] State ex rel. Freeman v. Scheve, 65 Neb. 853, 91 N.W. 846 (1902), rehearing, 65 Neb. 876, 93 N.W. 169 (1903).
[578] State ex rel. Finger v. Weedman, 55 S.D. 343, 226 N.W. 348 (1929).
[579] State ex rel. Clithero v. Showalter, 159 Wash. 519, 293 Pac. 1000 (1930), appeal dismissed, 284 U.S. 573 (1931); State ex rel. Dearle v. Frazier, 102 Wash. 369, 173 Pac. 35 (1918).
[580] State ex rel. Weiss v. District Bd. of Edgerton, 76 Wis. 177, 44 N.W. 967 (1890).
[581] Schempp v. Abington School Dist., 177 F. Supp. 398 (E.D. Pa. 1959), vacated and remanded, 364 U.S. 298 (1960), 201 F. Supp. 815 (E.D. Pa. 1962) appeal granted, 371 U.S. 807 (1962).

toleration cannot be taught without teaching religion."[582] In addition, these courts often took the position that it is for the legislature and the school boards, not the courts, to decide what books should be read in the schools, that if the Bible is read without comment, it can be read as great literature without raising questions about the truth of what is read, and that mere reading of the Bible does not amount to instruction in any religious faith. They argued that it is desirable that all children should read from the same books, that no sect should be given the right to veto what books should be read in the schools, and that Bible-reading helps to promote morality, one of the main objectives of education. "The noblest ideas of moral character," the Kansas court has noted, "are found in the Bible."[583] These courts also made much of the fact that comparable practices are found in state legislatures, state universities, prisons and other public institutions. "In fact," the Texas court once said, "Christianity is so interwoven with the web and woof of the State government that to sustain the contention that the Constitution prohibits reading the Bible, offering prayers, or singing songs of a religious character in any public building of the government, would produce a condition bordering upon moral anarchy."[584]

Ruling on this question in 1962, the Supreme Court of Florida declared that the issue of Bible-reading was related to the great struggle in the contemporary world between the competing systems of democracy and communism.[585] The Iowa court suggested, when it faced this issue a long time ago, that possibly the complaining party was a propagandist who regarded himself "charged with a mission to destroy the influence of the Bible," and observed that whether true or not the court had no such mission.[586] Finally, many of these courts ruled that no harm was done to those pupils who are excused from participation in the exercise.[587]

On the other hand, the judges who ruled that Bible-reading in the public schools constituted an illegal practice took the position that it is necessarily sectarian instruction, since all people are not Christians and since there are many differences among the various Christian sects. Thus, said the Wisconsin court, "the Bible contains numerous doctrinal passages, upon some of which the peculiar creed of almost every religious sect is based, and . . . such passages may reasonably be understood

---

[582] People ex rel. Vollmar v. Stanley, 81 Col. 276, 289, 255 Pac. 610, 616 (1927).
[583] Billard v. Board of Educ., 69 Kan. 53, 57, 76 Pac. 422, 423 (1904).
[584] Church v. Bullock, 104 Tex. 1, 7, 109 S.W. 115, 118 (1908).
[585] Chamberlin v. Dade County Bd. of Pub. Instruction, 143 So. 2d 21 (Fla. 1962).
[586] Moore v. Monroe, 64 Iowa 367, 370, 20 N.W. 475, 476 (1884).
[587] See Pfeiffer v. Board of Educ., 118 Mich. 560, 563, 77 N.W. 250, 253 (1898) ; People ex rel. Vollmar v. Stanley, 81 Col. 276, 293, 255 Pac. 610, 618 (1927).

to inculcate the doctrines predicated upon them."[588] Bible-reading without comment, especially if bracketed with prayer, is an act of religious devotion, these courts have held, and in fact carries the stamp of state approval. This does not mean that they desire to reflect adversely upon the great values of the Bible, the priceless truths of which are best taught in the churches, homes and religious schools. "The constitution does not interfere," the Wisconsin court has said, "with such teaching and culture. It only banishes theological polemics from the district schools."[589] Judges opposed to Bible-reading have usually defended the public schools, urging that they should always be equally available to all without any regard for religious differences. Thus it has been pointed out that there are differences considered to be important between the Douay and King James versions of the Bible, that the Jews accept only the Old Testament, and that any version of the Bible is sectarian for any non-Christian. Finally, it is argued that it is psychologically damaging to a child who is put in the position of a nonconformist by asking to be excused. This introduces a divisive influence into the public schools when one of their great values is that they tend to serve as a unifying force.

The Supreme Court at long last came to grips with this problem in June, 1963, when eight Justices joined in a decision holding that Bible-reading violated the first amendment, made applicable to the states through the due process clause of the fourteenth amendment.[590] This litigation involved a joinder of two cases, one involving a Pennsylvania statute, and one a rule made by the school board of Baltimore pursuant to statutory authority. In both instances, some verses from the Bible had to be read each day, without comment or discussion, and the Lord's Prayer was recited by the pupils in unison. Any child could be excused on written request of the parent or guardian. The main difference between the two cases was that the complaining parties in the Pennsylvania case were Unitarians, whereas in the Baltimore case they were atheists. The Pennsylvania practice was ruled invalid by a three-judge federal district court,[591] and the Baltimore rule had been upheld by the Maryland Court of Appeals by a four to three vote.[592]

---

[588] State ex rel. Weiss v. District Bd., 76 Wis. 177, 194, 44 N.W. 967, 973 (1890).
[589] State ex rel. Weiss v. District Bd., supra note 588, at 202, 44 N.W. at 976.
[590] Abington School Dist. v. Schempp, 374 U.S. 203 (1963). See Brown, Quis Custodiet Ipsos Custodes?—The School-Prayer Cases, 1963 Supreme Ct. Rev. 1; Kurland, The School Prayer Cases, The Wall between Church and State 142-79 (Oaks ed. 1962).
[591] Schempp v. Abington School Dist., 177 F. Supp. 398 (E.D. Pa. 1959), vacated and remanded, 364 U.S. 298 (1960), 201 F. Supp. 815 (E.D. Pa. 1962), appeal granted, 371 U.S. 807 (1962).
[592] Murray v. Curlett, 228 Md. 239, 179 A.2d 698 (1962), cert. granted, 371 U.S. 809 (1962).

Speaking for the Court, Justice Clark conceded that there were many evidences of the close identification of government with religion in the United States—chaplains and prayer in Congress and the armed services, and the like—but he also noted that religious freedom is strongly imbedded in our public and private life. He also called attention to the great religious diversity in this country, with 83 separate religious bodies having memberships in excess of 50,000, as well as innumerable smaller groups. Furthermore, said Justice Clark, certain legal principles are now firmly established, that the religious clauses of the first amendment apply fully to the states, that the contention that the establishment clause forbids only governmental preference of one religion over another has been rejected unequivocally by the Court, and that the establishment clause does not depend upon any showing of governmental compulsion. The Court's cases are committed, he declared, to a position of "wholesome neutrality" which "stems from a recognition of the teachings of history that powerful sects or groups might bring about a fusion of governmental and religious functions or a concert or dependency of one upon the other to the end that official support of the State or Federal Government would be placed behind the tenets of one or of all orthodoxies. This the Establishment Clause prohibits."[593] During the past twenty years the Court had considered the establishment clause in eight cases, and, Justice Clark wrote, the Court "has consistently held that the clause withdrew all legislative power respecting religious belief or the expression thereof. The test may be stated as follows: what are the purpose and the primary effect of the enactment? If either is the advancement or inhibition of religion then the enactment exceeds the scope of legislative power as circumscribed by the Constitution. That is to say that to withstand the strictures of the establishment clause there must be a secular legislative purpose and a primary effect that neither advances nor inhibits religion."[594]

The Court agreed with the finding of the three-judge federal district court in Pennsylvania that the opening school exercise, consisting of Bible-reading plus prayer, was a religious ceremony. As to the argument of the Maryland court that the purpose was to promote moral values, the Court's answer was that this purpose may not be pursued in public schools through the Bible, whose place as an instrument of religion could not be denied. The court also held that it was immaterial that students may be excused, since it is not necessary to show compulsion under the establishment clause. As for the argument that this was a relatively minor encroachment on the first amendment, the Court expressed agreement with Madison's warning that "it is proper to take

---

[593] 374 U.S. at 222.
[594] Ibid.

alarm at the first experiment on our liberties." Furthermore, Justice Clark denied that this decision, as alleged, sanctioned "a religion of secularism." Indeed, he pointed out that it would not be proper for the state to do that by affirmatively opposing or showing hostility to religion. He also made it clear that this decision did not forbid the study of comparative religion, or history of religion, or the Bible as literature and history. What the Constitution forbids is the holding of religious exercises in the public schools, for the first amendment requires that government "maintain strict neutrality, neither aiding nor opposing religion."[595] Finally, Justice Clark declared that this decision does not deny the majority's right to free exercise of religion; the free exercise clause has never meant that a majority may use the machinery of the state to practice its beliefs. The very purpose of the Bill of Rights was, in the quoted words of Justice Jackson, "to withdraw certain subjects from the vicissitudes of political controversy, to place them beyond the reach of majorities and officials and to establish them as legal principles to be applied by the courts."[596]

Justice Clark's closing paragraph is worth quoting: "The place of religion in our society is an exalted one, achieved through a long tradition of reliance on the home, the church and the inviolable citadel of the individual heart and mind. We have come to recognize through bitter experience that it is not within the power of government to invade that citadel, whether its purpose or effect be to aid or oppose, to advance or retard. In the relationship between man and religion, the State is firmly committed to a position of neutrality."[597]

Justice Douglas wrote a short concurring opinion to argue that the main objection to Bible-reading in these two cases is that the state thereby lends its assistance to a church's efforts to gain and keep adherents. Even in the absence of coercion, what was wrong here was, first, that the state was violating its required neutrality by conducting a religious exercise, and second, public funds and facilities were being used to give churches greater strength by promoting religious exercises. "The most effective way to establish any institution," said Justice Douglas, "is to finance it; and this truth is reflected in the appeals by church groups for public funds to finance their religious schools."[598] He put this sentence in italics, and I take it that the over-all purpose of his separate opinion was to argue that public aid to parochial schools is prohibited by the Constitution.

Justice Brennan filed a very lengthy concurring opinion covering 75

---

[595] Id. at 225.
[596] West Virginia Bd. of Educ. v. Barnette, 319 U.S. 624, 638 (1943), quoted 374 U.S. at 226.
[597] 374 U.S. at 226.
[598] Id. at 229.

pages of the *Reports*, and reviewing all phases of the problem, including all the precedents, in exhaustive detail. He found the *Engel* case controlling, and accepted the view that the establishment clause operates independently of the free exercise clause, and that limiting the establishment clause to Congress alone would deny us a viable religious liberty. He did not believe that the historical approach to construction of the first amendment was adequate, and that the whole question must be viewed in the light of contemporary circumstances, particularly those relating to the public schools and their "uniquely public function" of training American citizens in an atmosphere which is free from divisive influences. He thought that non-sectarian religious practices, equally with sectarian exercises, violate the establishment clause. And while he thought that a showing of coercion was not essential in a case dealing with establishment, he also felt that there was coercion in fact under the circumstances, since the pupil who asks to be excused must in effect make what his teachers and schoolmates are bound to regard as tantamount to a profession of disbelief. Young children, he said, are not likely to step out of line or flout peer-group norms.[599] Justice Brennan suggested, as a general formulation, that the establishment clause forbids "those involvements of religions with secular institutions which (a) serve the essentially religious activities of religious institutions; (b) employ the organs of government for essentially religious purposes; or (c) use essentially religious means to serve governmental ends, where secular means would suffice."[600] In suggesting that religious institutions may have nonreligious activities, and that religious means may perhaps be employed by government where secular means do not suffice, Justice Brennan has not only broken new ground, but has probably raised more new issues than he may have bargained for.

Justice Goldberg filed a brief concurring opinion, in which Justice Harlan joined, to stress that the two proscriptions relating to establishment and free exercise of religion must be read together since they are designed to serve a single end—"the fullest possible scope of religious liberty and tolerance for all . . . ."[601] But he said that for him no simple and precise line can be drawn between what is permissible and what is not permissible, and while he believed in the concept of neutrality, he warned against "untutored devotion" to the concept which might "partake not simply of that noninterference and noninvolvement with the religious which the Constitution commands, but of a brooding and pervasive devotion to the secular and a passive, or even active, hostility to the religious."[602] Nevertheless, he had no doubt concerning

---

[599] Id. at 289-92.
[600] Id. at 295.
[601] Id. at 305.
[602] Id. at 306.

the impropriety of the practices under discussion, for here there was "pervasive religiosity and direct governmental involvement inhering in the prescription of prayer and Bible reading in the public schools, during and as part of the curricular day, involving young impressionable children whose school attendance is statutorily compelled, and utilizing the prestige, power, and influence of school administration, staff, and authority . . . ."[603] This, he thought, went beyond mere accommodation.

Justice Stewart, who dissented alone, conceded that both the free-exercise and no-establishment clauses of the first amendment applied to the states through the fourteenth, but he thought it was "a fallacious oversimplification to regard these two provisions as establishing a single constitutional standard of 'separation of church and state,' which can be mechanically applied in every case . . . ."[604] In our free society, he said, it is necessary for government and religion to interact in countless ways, and he warned that a doctrinaire reading of the establishment clause leads to irreconcilable conflict with the free exercise clause. He argued that to ban religious exercises from the schools puts religion "at an artificial and state-created disadvantage," and constitutes "the establishment of a religion of secularism."[605] He also thought that mere reading of the Bible without comment did not constitute religious instruction, and he gave great emphasis to the absence of the element of coercion.

It is by no means true that the Regents' prayer and Bible-reading cases have brought the controversy over the place of religion in the public school to an end. This phase of American life is extremely complex, and the decided cases are direct authority only with regard to the specific situations which came to the Court for decision. Thus, to cite a recent example, the New York State Commissioner of Education ruled, on August 28, 1962, that a local public school board may not designate the fourth stanza of the "Star Spangled Banner" as a prayer to be recited daily as part of the opening exercises in the classroom. The commissioner decided that the fact that Francis Scott Key wrote these lines, and not public officials, was not decisive, the point being that a public school may not designate an official prayer, whatever its source. Of course, he said, our cherished National Anthem is entitled to our highest respect, and may be sung, or read, or recited, but officially-prescribed prayer is another matter. On the other hand, the corporation counsel for the school board of the District of Columbia ruled, on December 12, 1963, that public school pupils may sing Christmas carols

---

[603] Id. at 307.
[604] Id. at 309.
[605] Id. at 313.

during student assemblies and still be in harmony with the Supreme Court school prayer decision, so long as they are "incidental" and not a part of a religious exercise.[606] He also ruled that school officials may continue to invite clergymen to give invocations and benedictions at commencement exercises.[607] A New York court recently held that it was not unlawful for the school board to permit townspeople to erect a nativity scene on the school lawn at Christmas time, when the school was not in session, and where no public funds or employees were utilized.[608] At least two state courts have ruled that it was constitutionally improper to use the public schools for the distribution of the so-called Gideon Bible (the King James version of the New Testament plus the Psalms and Proverbs from the King James translation of the Old Testament), on the ground that this constituted preferential treatment of one religious sect over others.[609] On the other hand, there is no doubt of the legal propriety of purchasing Bibles for a public high-school library.[610] To note one more aspect of the problem, the highest court of the state of Washington ruled in 1918 that credit toward graduation may not be given in the public schools for religious instruction received outside the school.[611] On the other hand, several state attorneys general have ruled that it is quite proper, from a legal standpoint, for a school to give credit for a course on the Bible which is taught by a regular member of the school faculty.[612]

VII

I should like now to sum up. I have been concerned, in this essay, only with the public law aspects of the relationships which exist between state and church. I am well aware of the fact that even in the state-church area there is much more to be explored, such as the political and moral questions, to say nothing about the vast concern of religion with almost all branches of human experience. But I began with the assumption that we do live under a written Constitution which is the

---

[606] Washington Post, Dec. 13, 1963, Sec. B, p. 1.

[607] So the court ruled in State ex rel. Conway v. District Bd., 162 Wis. 482, 156 N.W. 477 (1916).

[608] Baer v. Kolmorgen, 14 Misc. 2d 1015, 181 N.Y.S.2d 230 (Sup. Ct. 1958).

[609] Brown v. Orange County Bd. of Pub. Instruction, 128 So. 2d 181 (Fla. Dist. Ct. App. 1960), cert. denied, 129 So. 2d 141 (Fla. 1961); Tudor v. Board of Educ., 14 N.J. 31, 100 A.2d 857 (1953), cert. denied, 348 U.S. 816 (1954), noted in 34 B.U.L. Rev. 375 (1954). The Attorney General of California ruled this way on June 10, 1955, 25 Cal. Ops. Atty Gen. No. 53/266.

[610] Evans v. Selma Union High School, 193 Cal. 54, 222 Pac. 801 (1924). The Attorney General of the State of Washington made a ruling to this effect on March 19, 1956.

[611] State ex rel. Dearle v. Frazier, 102 Wash. 369, 173 Pac. 35 (1918).

[612] Attorney General of Florida, June 23, 1948, 1947-1948 Atty. Gen. Report Florida 318, Op. No. 048-209; Attorney General of Alabama, Nov. 10, 1948, 1953 Ala. Atty. Gen. Report 68.

supreme law of the land, and that under our system of judicial review, its meaning is determined ultimately by the courts.

If we view church-state questions from this angle of vision, then we must start with the proposition that the first amendment guarantees the free exercise of religion and forbids Congress to pass laws respecting an establishment of religion, and that the fourteenth amendment made these guaranties applicable to the states. I am well aware of the fact that it has been argued that the liberty concept of the fourteenth amendment should be construed as absorbing only the free exercise part of the first amendment,[613] but the Supreme Court has repeatedly held that the no-establishment part also applies to the states, and I should suppose that by now this legal proposition is quite secure.

Furthermore, I have drawn attention to the fact that all state constitutions have provisions dealing with both the freedom of religion and the separation of church and state. Debate in the constitutional law field does not turn on whether these principles exist, but upon differing interpretations of the same general doctrines. Where a state decision is not controlled by state law grounds, then, of course, the state courts' construction of these principles is subject to correction by the United States Supreme Court. Thus in the *McCollum* case [614] the state courts ruled that the released time plan of religious education did not violate the provisions of either the state or federal constitution dealing with the separation of church and state. Accordingly, that left the federal question open, and on review the Supreme Court ruled that the local statute did violate the United States Constitution. In this connection it is important to note that the Illinois courts did not say that there is no such thing as separation, or that the principle is unimportant.

I have also argued that an analysis of statutory and case law clearly indicates that however important these principles may be, neither can be construed in any absolutistic way. There are limits to religious freedom, on the one hand, and the wall of separation is bound to be quite porous. As a matter of fact, I do not believe that religious thinkers claim that religious liberty is unlimited, though I must confess to a very limited acquaintance with theological writing. Thus in a very recent book, the Secretary for Religious Liberty of the World Council of Churches states categorically: "Some legal limitations of the exercise of religious liberty must be admitted as necessary and legitimate."[615] And the First Assembly of the World Council of Churches, which met in Amsterdam in 1948, said in its "Declaration on Religious Liberty":

---

[613] See, e.g., Snee, Religious Disestablishment and the Fourteenth Amendment, 1 Catholic Law. 301 (1955) ; Howe, Religion and Race in Public Education, 8 Buffalo L. Rev. 242 (1959).
[614] McCollum v. Board of Educ., 333 U.S. 203 (1948).
[615] De Albornoz, The Basis for Religious Liberty 150 (1963).

"The community has the right to require obedience to non-discriminatory laws passed in the interest of public order and well-being. In the exercise of its rights, a religious organization must respect the rights of other religious organizations and must safeguard the corporate and individual rights of the entire community."[616]

With some few exceptions, most scholars agree that freedom of religion and separation of church and state cannot be defined in absolute terms in the workaday world in which we live. The intellectual problem, the task of legislatures and courts, is to draw lines between what is licit and what is illicit, and obviously, we want these decisions to be made rationally and sensibly and not arbitrarily and quixotically. Certainly many attempts have been made to supply formulas which will serve as standards for the achievement of desirable results. Thus a very distinguished legal scholar has argued that what the first amendment really commands is that with respect to religion government must maintain "strict neutrality."[617] Similarly, Justice Clark said in his opinion in the recent Bible-reading case that "in the relationship between man and religion, the State is firmly committed to a position of neutrality."[618] I have no serious objection to this formulation since the concept of state neutrality responds to the constitutional command that government may neither prohibit the free exercise of religion nor establish religion. But the concept of neutrality does not solve the basic intellectual problem; I think it merely restates it. While it may be useful to say that the state is obliged to be neutral in matters of religion, this general formulation does not supply the solution to specific and concrete problems, such as whether bus rides to parochial schools constitute a departure from neutrality.

A competent scholar in a leading law school faculty has suggested the following test: "The freedom and separation clauses should be read as stating a single precept: that government cannot utilize religion as a standard for action or inaction because these clauses, read together as they should be, prohibit classification in terms of religion either to confer a benefit or to impose a burden."[619] I am afraid that this test oversimplifies the problem, and, at the same time, invites consequences which I would regard as unfortunate. Thus, under this test a statute which grants churches tax exemption, or exempts ministers or religious conscientious objectors from the obligation of military service, would be considered unconstitutional.[620] Even a statute authorizing the incorpora-

---

[616] De Albornoz, op. cit. supra note 615, at 159.
[617] Katz, Freedom of Religion and State Neutrality, 20 U. Chi. L. Rev. 426 (1953).
[618] Abington School Dist. v. Schempp, 374 U.S. 203, 226 (1963).
[619] Kurland, Religion and the Law 112 (1962).
[620] See Pfeffer, Religion-Blind Government, 15 Stan. L. Rev. 389 (1963).

tion of religious societies would, under this suggested test, be invalid. After all, as Justice Black remarked in the *Everson* case,[621] while the first amendment requires the state to be neutral, it does not require the state to be the adversary of religion or to handicap the religious.

I have also seen the suggestion that the test is whether, as regards freedom of religion or the separation of church and state, government has gone "too far."[622] While I agree that it is a wise prescription that government should not go too far, obviously such a simple formula does not help very much in trying to decide upon the merits of a particular course of action. A very learned legal scholar recently phrased a test for the public school aspect of this problem in the following language: " . . . for problems concerning religious intrusion in the public schools, the establishment clause of the first amendment is violated when the state engages in what may be fairly characterized as *solely religious activity* that is likely to result in (1) *compromising* the student's religious or conscientious beliefs or (2) *influencing* the student's freedom of religious or conscientious choice."[623] Again, while I regard this test as a useful contribution, I think that it merely restates the problem and does not solve it. After all, it would be no small task to spell out the ingredients of an improper influence upon the student's freedom of choice, or to decide when a student's beliefs have been compromised. And, as suggested by the Bible-reading cases, there is great dispute as to just what constitutes a religious activity.

In his recent book, Dean Drinan has pointed out that "no entirely satisfactory rationale for tax exemption has ever been stated in any American judicial decision."[624] I agree, but I would go further to say that this is equally true for most aspects of our problem. I do not believe that the problem can be solved, or even stated, in terms of simple formulas. Thus Dean Drinan is quite right, in my judgment, when he observes that the phrase "no-aid-to-religion" is an "enormous oversimplification," because in fact state and church in this country have been "friendly partners."[625] In fact, some theologians in this country now argue that church-state relations have become too intimate and too friendly, and that the amount of establishment now possible under prevailing constitutional law is too great and should be reduced.[626]

Obviously it does not help much merely to assert that the principles

[621] Everson v. Board of Educ., 330 U.S. 1, 18 (1947).
[622] Herberg, Religion and Education in America, Religious Perspectives in American Culture, 2 Religion in American Life 41 (1961).
[623] Choper, Religion in the Public Schools: A Proposed Constitutional Standard, 47 Minn. L. Rev. 329, 330 (1963).
[624] Drinan, Religion, the Courts, and Public Policy 9 (1963).
[625] Drinan, op. cit. supra note 624, at 35. See also Kauper, Church and State: Cooperative Separation, 60 Mich. L. Rev. 1 (1961).
[626] Berger, The Noise of Solemn Assemblies (1961).

of religious freedom and separation of church and state are not absolute, and that they cannot be reduced to simple formulas capable of ready and easy application in some automatic way. The question must still be faced: how do we go about deciding concrete cases? Clearly we have no legal slot-machines which will come up with the right answers if the proper buttons are punched. I know of no way of avoiding the use of rational judgment exercised in the light of all the factors of a particular situation. In an excellent analysis of this problem, a legal scholar recently suggested that we may at least approximate the underlying objectives of the first amendment "by carefully attending to the net effect of government activity, by giving attention to the real purpose of such activity when it produces multiple effects, by remaining sensitive to alternative means available to the civil process and obliging government to select those which impinge upon religion least . . . ."[627] In other words, in making specific judgments in concrete cases, I think we must eschew simplistic formulas, and analyze all the factors in the situation.

In doing so, however, we must bear in mind that the Constitution protects religious freedom and forbids establishments. This means that religious freedom is the rule, and that restraint is at best the exception to the rule. The burden of proof, therefore, is upon those who seek to justify restraint; religious freedom as such needs no special justification since it is specifically guaranteed by the Constitution, which, I remind you once more, is the supreme law of the law. Since the burden of proof is on those who seek to justify restraints upon religious freedom, I think it follows that all doubts must be resolved in favor of, and never against, this highly prized constitutional right. Of course, these rules of construction do not solve all problems, by any means, but such matters as the location of the burden of proof and the resolution of doubt, do in fact matter a great deal. They make a lot of difference in the conduct of our every-day affairs, and they weigh heavily in judicial calculation. Similarly, our constitutional law is committed to the separation of church and state, and here too doubts should be resolved in favor of the principle, and those who seek to justify climbing over the wall should be expected to carry a substantial burden of proof.

In resolving the doubts in church-state cases it is altogether proper and fitting that the judges should take into account the value judgments of legislators, and, for that matter, the predominant weight of public opinion. But it is equally important to remember that in our system of government the enjoyment of legal rights does not depend upon majorities or minorities: all people have the same rights. After all, the Constitution does not say that we shall enjoy as much religious freedom as

---

[627] Van Alstyne, Constitutional Separation of Church and State: The Quest for a Coherent Position, 57 Am. Pol. Sci. Rev. 864 (1963).

the current majority chooses to recognize; so far as constitutional rights are concerned, those who belong to the current majority have no better or greater rights than all the others. We have been reminded that "the Roman populace which cried 'To the lions with the Christians' were, of course, in the majority; so were the Spanish Inquisitors some 14 centuries later; and so were the French Bartholomew Day rioters a hundred years after that. When Peter Stuyvesant insisted that he wanted no 'Jews, Papists or Lutherans' in the new Dutch East Indies colony, he spoke for 'the majority'—as did all the other zealots who, in the name of God, heaped indignities on Baptists, Friends, Catholics and Jews throughout our colonial period."[628]

Perhaps it is worth pointing out that large areas of church-state relations are wholly noncontroversial. That there is a substantial consensus on many subjects should not be ignored or minimized. But in the area of controversy, I see no way out except to weigh the competing values, interests and considerations. If the issue relates to the propriety of a religious program in the public schools, for example, then we must take into account the educational value of the program, the impact upon nonparticipating students, the presence or absence of divisive side-effects, the possibility of discovering alternative programs which will accomplish the same objectives, the motives of those who push for the program, the additional burden upon the school system, and many other comparable questions. We must also remember that we must not so construe the no-establishment clause as to impair the value of the free exercise clause. Thus Justice Stewart recently reminded us that the guaranty of religious liberty "affirmatively requires government to create an atmosphere of hospitality and accommodation to individual belief or disbelief," and he went so far as to describe the Court's construction of the establishment clause as "insensitive and sterile."[629] For example, Justice Stewart argued that the Court's construction of the establishment clause not only permitted but required it to hold that a state may lawfully deny unemployment compensation to a worker who is not available for employment because he refuses on religious grounds to work on Saturday, for otherwise the state was favoring religion. While I do not believe that the Court's decisions have erected a wall of separation which is as high as Justice Stewart seems to think it has become, I do

[628] Jacobson, Should the Ayes Always Have It?, The Christian Century, Oct. 22, 1958. Cf. the remarks of Justice Jackson in West Virginia Bd. of Educ. v. Barnette, 319 U.S. 624, 638 (1943): "The very purpose of a Bill of Rights was to withdraw certain subjects from the vicissitudes of political controversy, to place them beyond the reach of majorities and officials and to establish them as legal principles to be applied by the courts. One's right to . . . freedom of worship . . . and other fundamental rights may not be submitted to vote; they depend on the outcome of no elections."
[629] Concurring opinion in Sherbert v. Verner, 374 U.S. 398, 414-16 (1963).

agree that in evaluating all the factors of a given situation, the potential conflict between the pull of the two parts of the first amendment must be taken into consideration.

I do not believe that the debate over church-state issues has reached an impasse, and this will not happen unless the extremists at both ends of the spectrum are permitted to take over. There is much room for accommodation and negotiation. In an important speech which he delivered on the floor of the Senate on May 20, 1963, Senator Ribicoff, who, it will be recalled, presided over the Department of Health, Education, and Welfare during the first two years of the Kennedy administration, pointed out: "For too long now the public debate has been dominated by the proponents of the extreme: those who want the federal government to finance private education exactly as it finances public education, and those who want no financial assistance to private education at all. . . . It is time the voices of thoughtful moderation were raised."[630] The Senator then proceeded to list a considerable number of negotiable items: income tax deductions for private school expenses; public financing of shared time, which means that children in private schools may be permitted to take some of their courses in the public schools, a proposal which I think may have merit;[631] assistance for earmarked purposes not related to religion, such as mathematics, science and foreign language teaching; teacher training programs; auxiliary services, such as school lunches, health services or bus transportation; and differentiation between higher education and education at the primary and secondary levels, a distinction already recognized in many items of federal legislation.[632]

A fruitful dialogue on church-state relations can be carried forward only in a spirit of moderation and restraint. One who believes that it is not the business of school authorities to write and prescribe prayers for the pupils is not necessarily irreligious or anti-religion or atheistic, and an atheist is not necessarily a Communist, even though Communists are likely to be atheists. We must guard against the temptation to bludgeon people into accepting religion. The late Zechariah Chafee once said: "Bribing men into a profession of faith is monstrous. Yet we may be moving that way. Frequent allusions to 'atheistic communism' are tending to identify free-thinking with disloyalty."[633] Similarly, the recent report of the Special Committee on Church and State of United Presby-

---

[630] Cong. Rec., May 20, 1963, pp. 8500-03 (daily ed.).

[631] See the symposium on shared time in Religious Education, Jan.-Feb. 1962.

[632] See the remarks of Justice Brennan in his concurring opinion in Abington School Dist. v. Schempp, 374 U.S. 203, 251-53 (1963), calling attention to the fact that there may be a legally significant difference between students considered from the point of view of age groupings. See also State ex rel. Sholes v. University of Minn., 236 Minn. 452, 54 N.W.2d 122 (1952).

[633] Chafee, The Blessings of Liberty 19 (1956).

terian Church made this point: "Debate on the issue of church-state relations is often blemished by irrationality and a tendency to estrange rather than to reconcile the groups that compose American communities. The branding of opponents of religious observance on public property as communists, the waging of telephone campaigns that invent and perpetrate slander, the evoking of racial and social fears, and the facile equation of 'Americanism' with 'Christianity' are the irrational accompaniments of much discussion of an issue whose solution demands unusual sobriety."[634]

Chief Justice Hughes, who was a devoted friend of civil liberty, once said that "the Constitution does not recognize an absolute and uncontrollable liberty. Liberty in each of its phases has its history and connotation. But the liberty safeguarded is liberty as a social organization which requires the protection of law against the evils which menace the health, safety, morals, and welfare of the people."[635] It is in this spirit, I believe, that we must seek to make our peace in those aspects of our constitutional law which are concerned with religion. Surely we can continue to live with a system which recognizes the broadest possible scope for religious freedom without ruling out the propriety of reasonable restraints upon that freedom where the legitimate and pressing purposes of society justify restraints. And I think that a complete and absolute separation between church and state, which permits no points of contact at all, is wholly unthinkable in our kind of civilization. It has been observed that "partial separation is an important principle not because it ends, but because it minimizes, conflict."[636] I suspect that this is about the best we can do.

---

[634] Relations between Church and State, A Report to the 174th General Assembly of the United Presbyterian Church in the United States of America, May, 1962 (Office of the General Assembly, Philadelphia, Pennsylvania), p. 8. Cf. the remarks in Ex parte Jentzsch, 112 Cal. 468, 471, 44 Pac. 803 (1896): "Liberty of conscience and belief is preserved alike to the followers of Christ, to Buddhist and Mohammedan, to all who think that their tenets alone are illumined by the light of divine truth; but it is equally preserved to the skeptic, agnostic, atheist, and infidel, who says in his heart, 'There is no God.'"
[635] West Coast Hotel Co. v. Parrish, 300 U.S. 379, 391 (1937).
[636] Beth, The American Theory of Church and State 135 (1958).